House Guest

A Thriller

Francis Durbridge

A SAMUEL FRENCH ACTING EDITION

FOUNDED 1830

SAMUELFRENCH-LONDON.CO.UK
SAMUELFRENCH.COM

FOR AMATEUR PRODUCTION ENQUIRIES

UNITED KINGDOM AND WORLD
EXCLUDING NORTH AMERICA
plays@SamuelFrench-London.co.uk
020 7255 4302/01

Each title is subject to availability from Samuel French,

depending upon country of performance.

HOUSE GUEST

First produced at the Yvonne Arnaud Theatre, Guildford, on 10th February, 1981

First presented in London by Michael Codron at the Savoy Theatre, London, on the 29th April 1981, with the following cast of characters—

Vivien Norwood	Jane Cussons
Jane Mercer	Sarah Bullen
Stella Drury	Susan Hampshire
Robert Drury	Gerald Harper
Crozier	Richard Gale
Inspector Burford	Philip Stone
Sergeant Clayton	Barry Stokes
Dorothy Medway	Barbara Atkinson
Philip Henderson	Ralph Greader

(Robert Drury and Philip Henderson were played by the same actor. "Ralph Greader" being an anagram of Gerald Harper)

The play directed by Val May
Setting by Graham Brown

The action takes place in the living-room of a house belonging to Robert and Stella Drury

ACT I   SCENE 1   Wednesday afternoon
        SCENE 2   An hour later
        SCENE 3   Wednesday night

ACT II SCENE 1   One a.m.
        SCENE 2   A few hours later
        SCENE 3   Thursday morning

Time—the present

FOR MARK...

ACT I

The living-room of a house near Weybridge, Surrey, England. Late afternoon in early spring

This is the home of Stella and Robert Drury. Although the house is large and stands in four acres the living-room is not enormous and has an unmistakable feeling of comfort and ease. There is a sofa, chairs, a large pouffe, a desk with a telephone on it, several tables with lamps and photographs. A bar, complete with attractive stools, takes up a corner of the room. A number of interesting pictures adorn the walls. A window with full length curtains, and sliding doors, opens on to a patio. Another door leads to the hall, the staircase, and the main part of the house. Opposite this door is the entrance to a room which is used as an office

When the CURTAIN *rises, Vivien Norwood is sitting on the sofa. There is a case on the floor by the side of her. After a while she glances at her watch, looks toward the hall, hesitates, then rises and goes to the open window. She is looking out of the window when Jane Mercer enters from the hall carrying a large envelope. Jane is ten years older than Vivien, but would hate to admit it*

Jane She'll be here in a minute. (*Offering the envelope*) Here's the photographs. There's several of the garden and a very good one of the pool and the summerhouse. If they're not what you want let me know and I'll see if I can find some others.

Vivien (*taking the envelope*) Thank you, Jane. You're my idea of the perfect secretary.

Jane I doubt it. I can type but my spelling's atrocious.

Vivien It can't be worse than mine. Anyway, I'm very grateful to you. I'm sure Mrs Drury only agreed to this interview because you said I was a friend of yours.

Jane You did me a favour—now I'm doing you one. (*Joining Vivien at the window*) Incidentally, when is this article of yours likely to appear?

Vivien Next month, I hope. Although, to be honest, they still haven't published the one I did on the Foreign Secretary's wife. They may well take it into their heads to do that first.

A pause

Jane Do you like the house?

Vivien I like it enormously—and I adore the bedroom. But tell me, just as a matter of interest, how on earth do they ever find each other in a bed that size?

Jane moves down to the sofa and sits on the arm

Jane I once asked Stella that very same question. She said "Robert's got a wonderful sense of direction." Of course, the house wasn't like this when they bought it. Robert spent a mint of money on it.

Vivien (*joining Jane*) I'm sure he did.

Jane (*indicating the office*) That side of the house was completely altered. That's where the garage used to be. The office was added later, when I joined them.

Vivien It's a terrific office.

Jane Yes—and there's a separate entrance, I don't know whether you noticed it or not. Which means, when things get too temperamental, I can sneak away without anyone knowing.

Vivien Does that often happen?

Jane No—to be truthful, not very often. And when it does, it's usually my fault.

Vivien When did they finally decide to return to England?

Jane About three years ago, but they'd been talking about it for some time. They were both tired of the States and they were worried about the boy; he was only six but he was getting completely out of hand. They just couldn't do anything with him. In the end they decided to settle over here and send him to Robert's old Prep School in Weybridge.

Vivien Smithson's?

Jane That's right. You've heard of it?

Vivien A friend of mine sent her son there. He was a little monster. It took two years and a mountain of money to turn him into an even bigger one.

Jane Well, that hasn't happened with Mike. It's done him the world of good. Robert's delighted with the progress he's made. And anyway, let's face it, Hollywood's no place to bring up children.

Vivien Not even if you happen to be Robert Drury?

Jane rises and crosses to the hall

Jane Especially if you happen to be Robert Drury.

Vivien sits on the sofa, picks up her case and opens it

Vivien How old did you say the boy was?

Jane Mike? He's nine.

Vivien (*placing the envelope in the case and taking out a portable tape-recorder*) Is he around? If he is, I'd like to talk to him. (*She puts the tape-recorder on a table*)

Jane No, he isn't around! And even if he was Stella certainly wouldn't let you interview him! That's why they left Hollywood, to get away from all that jazz. Anyway, he's in Rome at the moment. Robert had to go to Italy—there's some talk of him making a movie over there—and he took the boy with him. Robert's mother lives in Florence and like most grandmothers she's always complaining that she doesn't see enough of her grandson. They're due back next week.

Stella enters

Vivien rises

Stella (*to Vivien*) I'm sorry to have kept you waiting (*Before Vivien can reply*) Jane, you're going to be late for your appointment.
Jane I've plenty of time, Stella. By the way, before I forget. Mrs Jackson telephoned. She hopes to leave the hospital on Monday.
Stella Monday? That's sooner than we expected.
Jane Yes.
Stella That's very good news. (*To Vivien*) Mrs Jackson's our housekeeper. She's a marvellous woman.
Jane (*going to the office*) And an undisputed authority on haemorrhoids.

Jane exits

Stella smiles and sits on the pouffe

Stella (*indicating the sofa*) Do sit down, Miss . . .?
Vivien Norwood. Vivien Norwood.
Stella Well—how did you enjoy your conducted tour?
Vivien Very much. It's a lovely house. (*She sits on the sofa*)
Stella I'm glad you like it. We certainly enjoy living here. (*She suddenly notices the tape-recorder*) Oh, dear! You've got one of those wretched things! Incidentally, why on earth do you want to interview me? I haven't made a film in three years. It's my husband you should be interviewing.
Vivien We're concentrating on wives at the moment.

Vivien leans forward, arranges the tiny microphone and switches on the machine. Her manner is brisk and business-like

I hope you'll forgive me if I start by asking you a question I'm sure you've been asked many times before. Is it true that when you first met your husband you took an instant dislike to him?
Stella Yes, it is. I thought he was conceited, extremely rude, and very arrogant. In fact, we had a flaming row. But, contrary to general belief, I did not hit him over the head with a bottle of Scotch. It was Bourbon. The very next morning I had a cable from him which said, "Will definitely sue unless you have dinner with me every night next week". I ignored it and two days later a solicitor's letter arrived which said, "My client will settle for lunch".

Vivien laughs and adjusts the microphone, turning it more towards Stella

Vivien Tell me something, Mrs Drury. Everywhere you go you and your husband are made a fuss of. Certainly in Europe and the United States. Would it worry you very much if that didn't happen?
Stella (*surprised by the question*) If we were not made a fuss of?
Vivien Yes.
Stella I don't know. I've never really thought about it.
Vivien You mean—you both take that sort of thing for granted?
Stella Well—yes. I suppose we do. It can be irritating at times of course. Especially when you're dashing to the loo and someone waylays you for

your autograph. But, yes—I must be honest. I suppose we'd miss it terribly if it didn't happen. It's certainly nice to get V.I.P. treatment when you're flying off somewhere.

Vivien Jane tells me Mr Drury's in Rome at the moment, with your son.

Stella Yes, he is. There's some talk of us making another film with Mario Salvini. Although why on earth we should want to get involved with that megalomaniac again, I can't imagine.

Vivien He made *Life in the Sun* . . .

Stella That's right.

Vivien A wonderful film—and you were both super.

Stella Thank you.

Vivien Everyone said your husband should have got an Oscar.

Stella Not quite everyone.

Vivien Is this the first time Mike's been to Italy?

Stella It's the first time he's been to Rome. His grandmother—Robert's mother—lives outside Florence so naturally he's visited her several times.

Vivien Tell me a little bit about your son, Mrs Drury.

Stella What is it you want to know?

Vivien Did he have difficulty in adjusting?

Stella Adjusting? I'm not sure I know what you mean?

Vivien Well, take games, for instance. Does Mike play soccer?

Stella Yes, he does, and he adores it.

Vivien And cricket?

Stella He's not very good at cricket, I'm afraid. He horrified his father the other morning by calling it "upside-down" baseball.

Vivien laughs and prepares to ask the next question

Jane suddenly appears from the office

Jane Stella, Robert's here!

Stella (*amazed*) Robert! Already! (*Quickly, rising*) What a lovely surprise!

Stella moves towards the hall. Vivien rises and switches off the recorder

There is a pause, then Robert Drury enters. He is a good-looking man, but at this precise moment he appears tense and unmistakably weary

Robert! Darling, I wasn't expecting you back until . . . Where's Mike?

Robert slowly unbuttons his coat

Robert He's not with me, Stella.

Stella (*puzzled*) Not with you? (*Alarmed*) Why isn't he with you?

Robert (*hesitantly*) I'm afraid I've got some bad news. Mike's ill. I had to take him back to Florence and leave him with—Mother . . .

Stella Ill? What's the matter with him? (*Annoyed*) And what do you mean, you had to leave him with your mother? If he's ill you should have either brought him home or stayed with him!

Jane (*softly, with a low emphasis*) What's the matter with Mike?

Robert I'm not sure. It started with a cold, then he . . .

Stella Then he—what?
Robert Developed a temperature.
Stella Well, what is it? What's he got? You still haven't told us!

Robert does not answer; he just stands looking at her

    What does the doctor say?
Robert (*with almost a vague kind of tenseness*) They're not sure. They
    think . . . they just don't know.

*To Stella's surprise Robert turns away from her and, crossing to the bar,
proceeds to mix himself a drink. Stella looks at Jane, utterly bewildered*

Vivien (*embarrassed; indicating the tape-recorder*) I think perhaps we
    should postpone this interview, Mrs Drury, until one day next week.
    If—that's all right with you?
Stella (*staring at Robert; hardly aware of Vivien*) What? Yes . . . Yes, of
    course . . .

Vivien picks up the tape-recorder and puts it in her case. Robert turns

Jane (*in an attempt to lessen the tension*) This is a journalist friend of mine,
    Robert. Vivien Norwood.
Vivien I'm awfully sorry to hear about your son, Mr Drury. But I wouldn't
    worry too much if I were you. Children are quite extraordinary, you
    know, when it comes to illness. My little niece was terribly ill one
    Christmas and we all thought . . . (*Lamely realizing that Robert is taking
    no notice of her, but is staring at his wife*) They have great powers of
    recuperation—children . . .

Robert makes no comment

*Vivien looks across at Stella, as if wishing she had remained silent. She
hesitates, almost as if on the verge of saying something else, then changing
her mind she picks up her case and, with a little nod to Stella, goes out.
Jane follows her*

*The moment they have gone Robert puts down his drink and, quickly crossing
to Stella, takes her in his arms*

Robert Stella, listen!
Stella (*struggling*) Why didn't you send for me? Why didn't you phone?
    You know perfectly well that your mother will only try and make . . .
Robert Stella, listen! Please listen to me!

Stella stops struggling, arrested by the urgency in his voice

    Mike's not ill . . .
Stella (*releasing herself; staring at him*) Not ill?

Robert shakes his head

Robert He's been kidnapped.
Stella (*stunned*) Kidnapped? No! Oh, no!
Robert It's true, Stella.

Stella (*stricken*) My God—oh, my God . . . Where did this happen?
Robert In Rome.
Stella (*distraught*) What happened? Tell me what happened! Did you go
to the police?
Robert No, I didn't.
Stella You didn't! You didn't go to the police!
Robert No!
Stella (*flaring up; almost vehemently*) Why not? Surely that was the first
thing you should have done!
Robert (*hardly audible, obviously distressed*) Stella, for God's sake . . .! (*A
pause*) The past four or five hours have been unbearable. I kept going over
in my mind what I'd say to you. I knew it was no use lying, and yet the
thought of telling you the truth . . .
Stella You've got to tell me the truth! I've got to know what happened!

Robert leads Stella to the pouffe; he sits beside her, gently holding her arm

Robert Mike and I left Florence early on Monday morning. My mother,
of course, wanted him to stay with her whilst I was in Rome, but I knew
you wouldn't want that so . . . Anyway, we arrived at the hotel at about
two o'clock. My appointment with Mario was for three-thirty but I
didn't want to take Mike with me because—well, you know Mario.
Every other word is a four-letter word, he just can't help it. Mike was
excited at the thought of seeing Rome but he agreed to stay in the room
until I picked him up at about five o'clock. As it happened I was back in
the hotel by half-past four. The television was on and a bar of chocolate
was still on the arm of the settee—but there was no sign of Mike. At first
I wasn't too worried, I thought perhaps he'd gone downstairs to take a
look around. I was just about to go downstairs myself when I noticed
that a light was on in one of the wardrobes. When I looked inside I
discovered, to my amazement, that although my clothes were still intact,
Mike's things had disappeared. His overcoat, his underclothes, his
anorak, even the T-shirt with his name on it—they were all missing. I
don't have to tell you how I reacted. I panicked. And it was then that the
phone rang. (*Pause*) A man's voice said, "We have your son, Mr Drury,
and I suggest you meet a friend of mine at the Café Muralto on the Via
Veneto. Be there by nine o'clock". I was both frightened and angry and
all I could think of saying was, "Who the hell are you? And what
happens if I don't meet your friend?" He said, "I'll answer your first
question. My name is Crozier. The second question isn't worth answering
because you know, and I know that you'll be at that café long before
nine o'clock." (*After a moment*) And he was right, of course. I was
sitting in that bloody café, from seven o'clock until a quarter to ten. It
was sheer hell, Stella! Strangers kept coming up to my table asking for
my autograph—and all the time I kept saying to myself, "Is this the man?
Is this the bastard I'm waiting for?" Then, just as I was beginning to
think that no-one was going to contact me, a young Italian appeared
and handed me a shoe. It was Mike's. (*A tiny pause*) He said, "Your
boy is being well looked after, Mr Drury. But I must warn you, if you

go to the police, or report this incident to anyone—anyone at all—we shall have no alternative but to return the other shoe. Your son's foot will be inside it."

Stella slowly turns away from him and buries her head in her hands

I was stunned. I knew things like that did happen, especially in Italy, and yet I just couldn't believe it was happening to me. Finally, I said, "I'm not a wealthy man, but if you tell me what you want . . ." He said, "It isn't a question of money, Mr Drury. We want you to stay here, in Rome, until the day after tomorrow. That's important. After which you can return home, tell your wife what has happened, and wait."

Stella looks at him, puzzled

Stella Wait—for what?
Robert (*wearily*) I don't know, Stella . . .
Stella (*unable to control a note of hysteria*) But didn't you ask him what he meant?
Robert Of course I asked him! I never stopped asking him! But all he would say was, "Don't contact anyone. Not even your wife. Stay in your hotel until Wednesday morning, then return to England—and wait."
Stella This—this was on Monday? Monday night?
Robert Yes.
Stella Well—what happened yesterday?
Robert Nothing happened . . .
Stella What do you mean—nothing happened?
Robert I—I stayed in the hotel. I was scared—scared to hell of what they might do to Mike if I did otherwise.
Stella (*angrily*) You should have phoned me!

Robert rises, stands looking down at her

Robert Would you have telephoned *me*? Would you have taken that risk?
Stella I'd have done something!
Robert I did do something! I sat by the phone—all day—expecting the bastards to get in touch with me!
Stella You should have consulted the police!
Robert The Italian police? Do you know how many people are kidnapped —every month, every week, every day—in Italy?
Stella Then you should have got in touch with Scotland Yard—with McKenna. He's a good friend of ours. He'd have thought of . . .
Robert (*moving to the desk*) What could McKenna have done! And how would I have got in touch with him without anyone knowing? I've told you what happened at the café. The warning I received! ". . . If you go to the police, Mr Drury, or report this incident to anyone—anyone at all—we shall have no alternative but to return the other shoe." That wasn't just a threat, Stella. The bastard meant it! (*He sits in the chair at the desk*)

A tense pause

Stella (*with an effort*) Where do you think they've taken Mike?

Robert I don't know. I have a feeling he's no longer in Italy. That something happened yesterday; that he was taken somewhere. But whatever happened they're bound to get in touch with us sooner or later. They're bound to!

Stella But if it isn't a question of money . . .

Robert It must be a question of money! What else can they want? What else can we offer them?

Jane enters

Jane I'll cancel my appointment, Stella. You may need me . . .

Stella (*trying to conceal her emotion; not facing her*) No—no, don't do that!

Jane It's not important. I can easily . . .

Robert (*quietly, yet with authority*) Do what Stella says. Keep your appointment.

Jane Very well. (*After a moment*) Would you like me to have a word with your doctor? It occurred to me, perhaps if he spoke to your mother . . .

Robert (*sharply, cutting her short*) No—no, I don't want you to do that!

Jane (*puzzled, somewhat taken aback*) Yes, all right, Robert.

Robert (*relenting*) I shall be phoning myself later this evening.

A pause. Jane looks at Stella who is still turned away from her

We're just talking things over at the moment. Trying to make up our minds what to do. We'll let you know if there's any way in which you can help us.

Jane Well—try not to worry. I'm sure everything will be all right. I'll drop in later, on my way home.

Robert Yes. Yes—you do that, Jane.

Jane glances at Stella again, then goes out

A slight pause

Stella We shall have to tell her.

Robert No, we mustn't! We mustn't tell anyone . . .

Stella But supposing your mother phones and she takes the call?

Robert I'll talk to Mother tonight. I'll make up some story. I'll tell her Jane is away and we're spending the rest of the week at the cottage.

Stella But Jane is bound to get curious! She's bound to ask questions!

Robert Stella, for heaven's sake, don't let's worry about Jane!

Stella is both angry and near to tears as Robert rises, returns to the bar, and picks up his drink

Stella You shouldn't have left him . . .

Robert (*turning*) What do you mean—I shouldn't have left him?

Stella You shouldn't have left Mike in the hotel, you should have taken him with you.

Robert I couldn't take him with me!

Stella Why not?

Robert (*desperately on edge*) I've told you why not! You know what Mario's like. He only knows four-letter words.

There is a tense pause

Stella The man who telephoned you—what did you say his name was?
Robert Crozier.
Stella Was he English?
Robert I think so. (*Nodding*) Yes, I'm sure he was.
Stella And the other man, the Italian?
Robert He was about twenty-seven or eight. Dark. Good-looking. Spoke very good English.
Stella He said . . . (*She hesitates*)
Robert I've told you what he said, Stella!
Stella "Your boy is being well looked after"?
Robert Yes.
Stella You're sure he said that?
Robert Yes, I'm sure.
Stella You're not just saying that because . . .
Robert (*relenting*) No, Stella, I'm not! I promise you I'm not. That's what he said. (*With a slight Italian accent*) "Your boy is being well looked after, Mr Drury."

Jane enters

Jane (*to Robert*) There's someone to see you. He says he has an appointment.
Robert (*irritated by the interruption*) I haven't an appointment with anyone . . . (*He stops; looks at Stella*) Who is it?
Jane His name's Crozier.

Crozier appears from the hall. He wears a blazer and carefully pressed cavalry twill trousers. There are times when his public school accent does not quite ring true

Crozier I telephoned you, Mr Drury, while you were in Rome. If you don't remember my phone call I'm quite sure you recall meeting a friend of mine—Victor Endrico.
Robert I remember your phone call only too well—and your friend Victor. (*A moment*) Thank you, Jane.

Jane goes

Crozier turns and smiles at Jane as she goes out. Stella stares at Crozier almost as if she is in a state of shock. Pause

Stella (*softly, yet with fierce undertones*) Where's Mike? Where's my son? What have you done with him?
Crozier Your son has come to no harm, Mrs Drury, I assure you. There is no need for you . . .
Stella (*flaring at him*) Where is Mike? What have you done with him?
Robert (*quietly, trying to restrain her*) Stella . . .
Stella (*beside herself*) Where is he? Tell me! Tell me where he is!

Robert takes hold of her arm

Robert Stella, please! (*He moves quickly to the hall door and closes it*)

Crozier Your son is well. There's no need for you to be unduly worried. (*He looks at Robert*) Certainly not at this stage of the game.

Robert returns to Stella and faces Crozier

Robert What is your game, Mr Crozier?

Crozier Major Crozier. I'm glad you've asked that question because that's precisely why I'm here. To put you in the picture. (*He crosses to the study, opens the door, and peers inside to make sure the room is empty*)

Robert Well—before you start putting us in the picture, there's something you ought to know. Although I'm a well-known actor . . .

Crozier (*closing the door; moving to the sofa*) Don't be modest, Mr Drury. You're famous. You're a star.

Robert All right, I'm famous! But that doesn't mean I'm wealthy. So if you're labouring under the delusion . . .

Crozier (*making himself comfortable on the sofa*) Who said anything about your being wealthy? I thought Victor had made it quite clear that we're not holding your son to ransom.

Robert (*aggressively*) Then what are you doing? What is it you want?

Crozier Don't be disagreeable, my dear fellow. I'm quite prepared to tell you what I want. I want to stay here, in this house, for the next forty-eight hours. That is—tonight and tomorrow night. Then, if all goes well, I shall take leave of you both on Friday afternoon.

Stella (*to Crozier, quietly incredulous*) Is that all you want from us? Just—to stay here . . .?

Crozier That's all, Mrs Drury. Nothing else. Nothing else, I assure you. In return for your hospitality your son will be released.

Stella When?

Crozier On Friday. If all goes well, a car will pick me up on Friday afternoon. Mike will be in the car.

Stella looks at Robert, an unmistakable expression of relief on her face

Robert That's the second time you've said "if all goes well" . . .

Crozier It's a habit of mine, Mr Drury. Take no notice of it. Well—what do you say?

Robert Why do you wish to stay with us?

Crozier You're a very distinguished actor, you have a lovely house, a charming wife. Who wouldn't want to spend a few days in such delightful surroundings.

Robert Don't give me that bullshit! Answer the question!

A tense pause

Crozier (*to Stella*) I do wish you'd persuade your husband to be a little less aggressive. You have a very nice little boy, but not unnaturally he's feeling somewhat homesick at the moment. We'd like to return him to you as soon as possible.

Robert You still haven't answered my question! Why do you wish to stay here?

Crozier rises and looks at Robert, quietly sizing him up

Crozier I can see you're an obstinate man who's used to getting his own way. Unfortunately I'm an obstinate man too. (*With an air of finality*) I've told you what I want—now it's up to you.

Robert (*angrily*) It's as simple as that?

Crozier As simple as that.

Stella Is that really all you want from us—just to stay in this house for the next forty-eight hours?

Crozier That's all, Mrs Drury. Nothing else. (*Pause. To Robert*) Well—what do you say? Am I to be your guest?

Stella looks at Robert and gives a frightened little nod

Robert First things first, Major Crozier.

Crozier What does that mean?

Robert It means that first, before anything else, I must have proof—definite proof—that Mike is still alive.

Crozier My dear fellow, of course he's alive!

Robert I want proof.

Crozier Would I be here if he wasn't?

Robert I want proof.

A pause

Crozier I rather thought you would, Mr Drury. Your son is alive and in England. A friend of mine took a photograph of him this morning—soon after he arrived.

Robert Photographs can be faked.

Crozier They can. They can indeed. But this one happens to be genuine.

Crozier moves nearer the window and beckons to someone outside. A pause

Vivien enters. She is carrying her case

Robert and Stella stare at her in amazement

Show them your photograph.

Vivien moves down to the sofa and quietly opens her case. She takes out a photograph which she hands to Crozier. He glances at it, then passes it to Robert. A pause. Robert and Stella stare at the photograph

Robert (*quietly, to Vivien*) This was taken this morning?

Vivien Yes, it was—near Dover.

As Robert and Stella continue staring at the photograph

If you look carefully you can see a signpost on the right of the lorry . . .

Stella Is that how Mike was brought back? Hidden in a lorry!

Crozier He was asleep most of the time and quite comfortable, Mrs Drury, I assure you.

Another pause

Robert (*looking up from the photograph*) If I go along with what you

suggest—if I let you stay here for the next forty-eight hours—we have your assurance that Mike will be returned to us?
Crozier I've already told you that.

Robert hesitates. Stella takes hold of his arm. She realizes only too well that her husband is not used to taking orders from anyone

Stella (*worried*) Robert . . .

A brief pause

Robert Very well. I agree. On one condition . . .
Crozier There are no conditions. Except the ones I make. (*To Vivien, with authority*) You've seen the house?

Vivien nods

Which room?
Vivien I think you'd be well advised to occupy a room on the far side of the house. There's a separate staircase.
Crozier Is there a phone?
Vivien Yes.

Crozier nods

Crozier (*dismissing her*) My suitcase is in the boot of the car, take it upstairs and stay with it! (*He hands her the car keys*)

Vivien looks at Robert, then goes out into the hall

Crozier (*to Robert*) I shall want a key to the front door. See that I get one. (*Turning to Stella*) Apart from your housekeeper I believe you employ a daily woman—a Mrs Porter.
Stella Yes.
Crozier According to my information Mrs Porter is an excellent worker but something of a gossip. Would you go along with that description?

Stella looks at Robert, hesitates, then gives Crozier a little nod

Then I'd like you to dispense with the good lady's services, let's say—until next Monday morning. I suggest you tell her you're going down to your cottage for the rest of the week.
Robert You appear to be unusually well informed about our affairs. Who told you about the cottage?
Crozier (*ignoring the question*) That leaves your secretary Miss Mercer. (*A brief pause*) Since Miss Mercer and I will inevitably be bumping into each other from time to time I think perhaps—(*Giving the matter thought*)—you should tell her the truth.
Robert The truth being that you've kidnapped Mike and that you're blackmailing me?
Crozier That's right, my dear fellow. (*With a little nod*) You have my permission to tell her the whole story. Right from the beginning. But please, don't forget to warn her. (*Pause*) If Miss Mercer talks—if she goes to the police—we shall have no alternative but to return the other shoe. Your son's foot will be inside it.

Crozier looks at Stella, then turns and exits into the hall

The Lights fade as—

> *the* CURTAIN *falls*

SCENE 2

The same. About an hour later

When the CURTAIN *rises a tired, distraught Stella is standing by the bar. She quickly turns as Robert enters from the hall*

Stella What's happening?
Robert They're still talking.
Stella They must have been upstairs the best part of an hour.

Robert nods

What are they talking about?
Robert I'm not sure. I daren't get too near the room in case they hear me. I have the impression he wants her to stay the night and she's trying to talk herself out of it.
Stella (*in a tense whisper, as if frightened of being overheard*) Do you think Crozier was telling the truth when he said they'd release Mike the day he leaves here?
Robert (*thoughtfully, his eyes on the hall*) I honestly don't know. I don't know whether he was telling the truth or not. (*He moves down to Stella*)

Pause

Stella Robert, you know what we were saying about Jane.
Robert Yes.
Stella It seems absurd, I know, but—I can't get away from the fact that it was Jane that brought that girl here. Apart from which, Crozier seems to know so much about us. He knew about Mrs Porter, about the cottage. Someone must have talked to him.
Robert How long has Jane been friendly with this Norwood girl?
Stella I have a feeling she hasn't known her very long.
Robert When did Jane first mention her to you?
Stella The day you left. She said she had a friend who badly wanted to interview me. I wasn't too happy about it, but she said the girl—Vivien Norwood—had done her a favour and she'd be grateful if I'd see her, if only for ten minutes.
Robert Did she tell you what the favour was?
Stella No, and I didn't ask her. As soon as they arrived Jane asked me if she could show her over the house. It seemed a perfectly natural request at the time, but I realize now, of course . . . (*She stops; gives a startled look towards the hall*)

Robert has also heard a noise and quickly turns. Pause

Robert (*looking into the hall*) It's the girl! She's coming down! Leave us,
  Stella! ·
Stella (*puzzled*) Leave you?
Robert Yes, leave me alone with her.
Stella Why? What are you going to do?
Robert I want to talk to her—on my own.

Stella looks at him

  Please do as I say! Leave me!

Stella hesitates, then goes quickly into the office

Pause

  Vivien enters

Vivien I believe Major Crozier asked you for a front door key.

*Robert stares at her for a moment, then takes a key out of his pocket and
offers it to her*

  (*Taking the key*) Thank you. I'm leaving now but I'll be back about ten.
  I shall be staying the night. (*Quietly, yet with authority*) Before I go I'd
  like to give you a piece of advice.
Robert Go ahead. I could certainly use some advice right now.
Vivien Don't underrate Crozier. He can be both difficult and ruthless.
Robert Is that your advice?
Vivien Yes.
Robert Then there's no problem. I'm already sold on that, I assure you.
Vivien I warn you. Whatever you do, don't try and cross him.
Robert Why should I try and cross him? All I'm interested in is the safety
  of my son.
Vivien At the moment your boy is being well looked after. But if the
  situation changes, if you or your wife suddenly decide to do something
  stupid . . .
Robert You mean—send for the police?
Vivien That would be very stupid. But that's not what I meant.
Robert What did you mean?
Vivien I meant, if any of your friends decide to call on you during the next
  forty-eight hours don't—under any circumstances—arouse their
  suspicion. If they happen to see Crozier simply introduce him as a
  business associate and leave it at that. He'll take care of the situation.
Robert I'm sure he will. Are there any other instructions?
Vivien Yes. He'll be making several phone calls. (*Indicating the telephone*)
  Don't, I beg you, attempt to eavesdrop. However much you may feel
  tempted to do so.
Robert Miss Norwood, I'm interested in one thing and one thing only.
  My son. So far as I'm concerned Colonel Crozier, or Major Crozier, or
  what the devil he calls himself, can live on the telephone! I just couldn't
  care less.
Vivien (*with the first suggestion of a smile*) I think we understand one another.

Robert (*looking at her*) I think perhaps we do. In which case, would you be kind enough to tell me something?

Vivien I might. What is it you want to know?

Robert (*moving nearer to her; with a friendly note in his voice*) Has your friend the slightest intention of keeping his word? Will he release Mike the day he leaves here?

Vivien (*after a tiny hesitation*) Yes—providing you play ball with him.

Robert Aren't we doing that already, by letting him stay with us? (*When she does not answer him*) Or is there something else he wants?

Vivien Major Crozier has already answered that question.

Robert He simply wants to stay here, in this house for the next forty-eight hours?

Vivien That's right.

Robert There's nothing else he wants from us?

Vivien (*again with a slight hesitation*) Nothing.

Robert Because if there is, now's the time to tell me.

Vivien There's nothing else. (*She glances at her watch*) Are there any more questions, Mr Drury?

Robert Where is Mike now? Where have you taken him?

Vivien You know perfectly well I can't answer that question.

Robert Can't—or won't?

Silence

Do you know where he is?

Vivien (*after a moment*) Yes, I know. But all I can tell you is, he's being well looked after, and there's nothing for you to worry about. Not at the moment.

Robert Not at the moment?

Vivien (*after a tiny hesitation; avoiding looking at him*) I'm sorry for you and your wife. Kidnapping the boy wasn't my idea.

Robert is quietly projecting his personality and she, raising her eyes, gives him a long look. He moves slightly nearer her

Robert I believe that.

Vivien If I could help you in any way, I would.

Robert I believe that too.

Vivien (*suddenly cold and unfriendly*) But I can't! So switch off the Hollywood charm, Mr Drury—and get off the set!

Vivien exits

Robert stares after her, completely taken aback

There is a pause, then Stella comes out of the office

Robert (*turning*) Did you hear that?

Stella Yes, I heard.

Robert (*smarting from Vivien's remark*) The bitch! The arrogant little bitch! All right, Stella, you don't have to tell me! It didn't work!

Stella (*desperately worried*) What are we going to do?

Robert (*fiercely*) I don't know. (*He goes to the bar, reaches for a bottle, then hesitates*) I feel so angry! So damned angry! (*Pause*) Maybe I was wrong. Maybe I should have contacted Superintendent McKenna.

Stella No, I don't think you were wrong. Not the way things have turned out. I was annoyed at first because you didn't go to the police, but I realize now it would have been a mistake. Don't reproach yourself. You did the right thing.

Robert (*controlling a note of desperation*) I'll do anything—just anything to get Mike back! I promise you.

Stella I know that. So would I.

The doorbell rings. They both turn and look towards the hall

Robert It's probably Jane. I expect she's forgotten her keys.

Stella If it is—what are we going to tell her?

Robert Before we tell her anything we'll question her about Vivien Norwood.

Stella gives a little nod and goes into the hall

A pause. Robert picks up the bottle. He is about to mix himself a drink when voices are heard

Burford (*off, in the hall*) I'm very sorry to disturb you, Mrs Drury. But we'd very much like to have a word with your husband. It is important, ma'am.

Stella (*off*) Well—please come this way.

Stella enters with Inspector Burford and Clayton, a uniformed sergeant. Burford is a rather heavily built man in his early fifties. He carries a well-worn attaché case

(*With near panic in her voice*) It's the police, Robert! They want to talk to you!

Burford (*after a glance at Stella*) My name is Burford, Mr Drury. Detective Inspector Burford. Surrey C.I.D. I think you know Sergeant Clayton, sir.

Clayton (*grinning*) Kingston Hill, sir.

Robert Kingston Hill?

Clayton Speeding, sir. You got away with it. My colleague was a fan of yours.

Robert Ah, yes. (*Moving down to them*) It depends what you mean by "got away with it", Sergeant. It was in the *News of the World*.

Clayton There was nothing we could do about that, sir.

Burford I believe you have a cottage in Dorset, Mr Drury. Near Lyme Regis?

Robert (*surprised by the question*) Yes, that's right.

Burford When did you last visit the cottage, sir?

Robert Oh—about four or five weeks ago. (*He looks at Stella for confirmation*)

Stella (*puzzled*) It was four weeks last Saturday.

Robert Why? Has something happened?

Burford (*ignoring the question*) Who looks after the place, sir, when you're not there?

Robert Strictly speaking, no-one looks after it. A cousin of mine lives locally. She has a set of keys and drops in from time to time.

Burford Would that be Miss Medway?

Robert Yes, that's right. Dorothy Medway. (*Puzzled*) What is it? What's this all about?

Burford Miss Medway called in the cottage early this morning. There was no sign of a break-in but, to her amazement, she came across the body of a dead man.

Robert Good God!

Burford The body was in the living-room, near the fireplace. The man was about twenty-seven or eight. Apparently a stranger to the district. Certainly Miss Medway had never seen him before.

Stella How did he die?

Burford He was murdered, Mrs Drury. Stabbed to death. (*He opens his case and takes out a long, narrow object, which has been carefully wrapped in a towel*) This is the murder weapon. I'd like you both to take a good look at it.

Burford slowly removes the cloth, revealing a large, ornamental dagger. It is immediately obvious to him that both Robert and Stella have seen the weapon before

(*Quietly*) I take it you've seen this before, sir?

Robert Yes, of course I have! It's mine. But surely Dorothy—Miss Medway—must have told you that?

Burford (*nodding*) She said it was usually kept over the bookcase in the living-room.

Robert That's right. It was.

Burford When did you last see it, sir?

Robert When I last visited the cottage.

Burford (*looking at him*) About four or five weeks ago?

Robert (*a shade irritated*) My wife told you when it was. It was four weeks last Saturday.

A tiny pause. Burford looks at the dagger

Burford It's an impressive looking dagger, sir. I've seen several in my time. In fact, a colleague of mine used to collect them—but I've never seen one quite like this before.

Clayton (*to Burford*) It's what's known as a "Rondel" dagger, Inspector.

Burford looks at Clayton

Robert That's correct. It is. It's called "Rondel" because of the handle.

Burford How did you come by it, Mr Drury?

Robert About seven years ago I made a film in Santa Marco.

Burford Santa Marco?

Clayton That's in Mexico, sir.

Burford (*with a look*) Thank you, Sergeant.
Clayton Near Acapulco.

Burford gives him another look

Robert The dagger was used in the film and since I rather admired it the
  producer very kindly made me a present of it when the film was finished.
Burford I see. (*He wraps the dagger in the cloth and puts it down. A slight
  pause*) I'd like you to give me an account of your movements, Mr Drury,
  during the past day or so.
Robert I've been abroad for the last ten days, on the Continent. I only got
  back this afternoon.
Burford From where, sir?
Robert From Rome.
Burford Rome? How long were you in Rome, sir?
Robert (*hesitating*) Oh—about forty-eight hours.
Burford Only forty-eight hours? Quite a short visit.
Robert (*a shade uneasily*) Yes, it was.
Burford Which hotel did you stay at?
Robert The *Excelsior* . . .
Burford Do you, by any chance, remember the number of your room?
Robert (*surprised by the question*) Yes, of course I do! But I fail to see what
  the devil . . .
Burford (*stopping him*) Was it three-oh-nine? Suite three-oh-nine?
Robert (*staggered*) Yes—it was.
Stella How on earth did you know that?
Burford We found an envelope on the dead man, Mrs Drury. Someone,
  presumably the man himself, had scribbled various notes on it. (*To
  Robert*) Your initials—R.D.—were on the back of the envelope,
  together with the words "Excelsior—Suite three-oh-nine".

*Robert makes no comment. Stella stares at him, both puzzled and deeply
worried. Burford eyes them both with interest*

  You say you were abroad for ten days?
Robert Yes. We left Florence on Monday morning. I had an appointment
  in Rome with a film producer called . . .
Burford "We" sir?
Robert (*after a moment*) My little boy was with me . . .
Stella Robert's mother lives near Florence and they'd been staying with
  her.
Burford Oh, I see. Go on, sir. You were about to say . . .
Robert I was about to say I had an appointment in Rome with a film
  producer—Mario Salvini.
Clayton *Life in the Sun?*
Robert That's right, Sergeant.
Burford (*after a glance at the Sergeant*) Did you have any other appoint-
  ments, sir?
Robert No.
Burford You didn't see anyone else whilst you were in Rome?

Robert No, I didn't. That is—no-one of importance.
Burford Let me be the judge of that.

A pause. They look at one another steadily

You didn't, by any chance, meet an Italian called Victor Endrico?

Stella gives a little start of surprise. Burford is aware of this, but he quite deliberately refrains from looking at her

Robert (*not very convincingly*) Who is Victor Endrico?
Burford He's the young man that was stabbed to death in the living-room of your cottage.
Robert (*after an awkward pause*) What makes you think I might have met him? Because of what was on the envelope?
Burford Partly that, sir. And partly the fact that—by a strange coincidence —he was also in Rome, whilst you were there.
Robert Well, what on earth does that prove? It certainly doesn't prove that I knew the man!
Stella How do you know he was in Rome, Inspector?
Burford The envelope wasn't the only thing we found on him, Mrs Drury. We found his passport and an airline ticket.
Robert Well—I'm sorry I can't help you. (*He avoids looking at Burford*) I've never heard of anyone called Victor Endrico. Why he should have had my initials and room number on the back of an envelope I just can't imagine.
Burford Can't you, sir? Well, perhaps Mrs Drury has more imagination than you. Perhaps she can help us.

Burford slowly turns towards Stella. Pause. Stella is worried and a shade desperate. She would dearly love to avoid Burford's steady gaze, but for some curious reason she finds herself unable to turn away from him

Mrs Drury, it's perfectly obvious to me that both you and your husband knew Victor Endrico. You knew that he'd been murdered and yet you both deliberately . . .
Stella (*quickly; almost a cry of despair*) No! No, that's not true! It's just not true, Inspector!

Robert hesitates, then moves to his wife and gently takes hold of her. There is a pause

Robert (*to Burford*) My wife's desperately worried, Inspector. We both are. (*After a moment, with an air of finality*) Whilst I was in Rome our son—Mike—was kidnapped.
Burford Kidnapped! Is this true, Mrs Drury?

Stella nods

Robert Shortly after he disappeared I received a telephone call from a man calling himself Major Crozier. He told me, warned me in fact, not to go to the police. Instead—he told me to meet a friend of his at café on the Via Veneto.

A slight pause

Burford Go on, sir.

Robert I went to the café and I met his friend. It was Victor Endrico.

Burford (*after a moment*) Was this the first time you'd met Endrico?

Robert Yes, of course it was! It was the only time—and I've never seen him since!

Burford Go on, sir.

Robert I don't have to tell you how I felt. I was desperately worried; frightened in fact. I offered Endrico money but he simply shook his head and said it wasn't a question of money. When I asked him what he wanted he told me to stay in Rome until Wednesday morning, this morning that is, then to return home—and wait.

Burford Wait for what, sir?

Robert He didn't say. But shortly after I arrived home the man who telephoned me—Major Crozier—put in an appearance. He too assured me that it wasn't just a question of a ransom. He said he simply wanted to stay here, in this house, as our guest. He said if we agreed to this Mike would be returned to us—unharmed.

Burford gives Robert's story thought

Burford I don't understand this. Why should this man want to stay here with you and Mrs Drury? And where is he now, this Major Crozier?

Robert He's upstairs in one of the guest rooms.

Burford turns and looks towards the hall

Burford How long has he been here?

Robert Since about five o'clock.

Burford Is he alone?

Robert Yes. There was a girl with him, but she left just before you arrived. She's returning later.

A pause—then Burford makes a decision and turns towards Stella

Burford I want you to go upstairs and tell this Major Crozier that the police are here, and that they would very much like to have a word with him. Say that your husband had to admit that there was a guest staying in the house and that he's described Major Crozier as a close friend. Don't say anything else, Mrs Drury. Don't answer any questions. If you don't return almost immediately Sergeant Clayton and I will fetch you.

Stella looks at Robert, hesitates, then goes out

Clayton moves down to Robert. They stand staring into the hall. Pause

You say there was a girl with Crozier?

Robert Yes. A journalist. Vivien Norwood. At least, she calls herself a journalist.

Clayton Norwood?

Burford Do you know her, Sergeant?

Clayton (*to Robert*) A dark, rather good-looking girl? Trendy?

Robert Yes, I suppose that's how you'd describe her.

Clayton I don't know her. But she dropped in the Station about a month ago. (*Thoughtfully*) It had something to do with her car ... (*Suddenly*) I remember! She thought her car had been towed away, but it turned out she'd forgotten where she'd parked it.

Burford (*to Robert*) Did she arrive with Crozier?

Robert No, she was already here.

Burford How did that come about, sir?

Robert She was interviewing my wife for some magazine or other. At least, that was her excuse.

Burford But there's no doubt in your mind—none whatsoever—that she's in league with Crozier?

Robert No doubt. (*He stares anxiously into the hall*)

Burford (*to Clayton; with a little nod*) Then it's ten to one she knew Endrico. (*A brief pause*) Mr Drury, may I use your desk?

Robert Yes, of course.

Burford goes to the desk, sits down, and takes out a notebook and pen. There is a pause while he studies the notebook, finally writing something on one of the pages. He starts reading what he has written

Clayton Here's Mrs Drury!

Burford rises and rejoins Robert and Clayton near the hall

Stella enters

Stella (*quietly moving into the room*) He was on the phone. He's coming down.

Robert What did he say?

Stella He asked me who it was. He'd heard the bell. I said it was the police.

Burford What was his reaction?

Stella I don't really know. I spoke to him through the door. (*To Robert*) I said you'd told the Inspector he was a business associate and that we'd invited him to stay with us for two or three days.

Robert nods

Burford That's fine. Thank you, Mrs Drury. (*To Robert*) Now leave this to me, sir.

Clayton (*to Stella, indicating the sofa*) Mrs Drury ...

Stella crosses and sits on the sofa. Clayton stands behind her, his eyes on the hall. Pause

Crozier enters. He has put on a dressing-gown

Burford (*pleasantly*) Good evening, sir. I'm Inspector Burford. I'd be grateful if you'd spare me a few minutes.

Crozier Yes, of course, Inspector. But what's this all about?

Burford I'm investigating a murder case, sir—and I was wondering if by any chance ...

Crozier A murder case! (*He looks at Robert, then at Burford again. Quietly*) Who's been murdered, Inspector?

Burford A young man called Victor Endrico.
Crozier Victor . . . ?
Burford Endrico.
Crozier The name sounds Spanish.
Burford He was an Italian, sir. His body was found in a cottage near Lyme Regis. The cottage belongs to Mr Drury—which is why I'm here, Major.
Crozier Good heavens! Did you know this man, Robert?
Robert No. No—I'd never heard of him until the Inspector arrived.
Crozier (*to Burford; almost with authority*) Well—what happened exactly?
Burford We don't know what happened, sir. That's what we're trying to find out.
Crozier Yes, but surely . . . I mean, obviously he broke into the cottage, so you must have some idea . . .
Burford No, sir! He didn't. There was no sign of a break-in.
Crozier Really? Then how the devil did he get in? Had he a key?
Burford We didn't find one on him, sir. (*After a moment, studying Crozier*) Have you ever been to the cottage, Major?
Crozier Me? No, I'm afraid I haven't.
Burford I thought perhaps being a friend of Mr Drury's you might have spent the odd weekend down there.
Crozier No. Robert has invited me down there, several times, but I've always cried off, I'm afraid. (*Smiling at Stella*) Country life doesn't appeal to me. But tell me a little more about this Italian chap, Inspector. How was he murdered? Was he shot?
Burford No. He was stabbed to death. (*He picks up the dagger and unwraps it*) With this, sir.
Crozier Good God!
Burford It belongs to Mr Drury. A friend of his—a film producer—gave it to him. It wasn't you, by any chance, sir?
Crozier No, I'm afraid it wasn't. And in answer to the question you're just about to ask me: I've never seen it before.
Burford (*smiling*) Thank you, sir.
Crozier If it belongs to Mr Drury, how did the murderer get possession of it?
Robert (*quietly, looking at him*) It was hanging on the wall, in the living-room of the cottage.
Crozier Oh. Oh, I see.
Burford And very decorative it must have looked. It's what's known as a "Rondel" dagger. That's right, isn't it, Sergeant?
Clayton That's right, sir.
Burford Mexican, I think you said, Mr Drury?
Robert It was given to me in Mexico. I don't really know where it came from.
Crozier Well—it's certainly a very handsome looking weapon.
Burford It is indeed, sir.

Suddenly, and with tremendous agility, Burford leaps forward and plunges the dagger into Crozier's body. At precisely the same moment Clayton grabs Stella by the wrist. In a split-second there is a flick-knife in his hand and he is leaning over Stella, holding the knife terrifyingly near her throat. Robert is thunderstruck, and for a moment utterly speechless. He stares at Burford in amazement, then at the terrified Stella—finally at the dead man

(*fiercely*) Pick up the dagger!
Robert Who are you? Who the hell are you?
Burford You heard what I said! Pick it up!

Robert continues to face Burford, then he turns and looks at Stella again. There is a pause—finally he stoops down and slowly picks up the dagger. Another pause. Robert stares at the weapon and the blood on his hands

Okay. Now drop the dagger and go over to the phone.
Robert (*suddenly pulling himself together*) First—you tell that son-of-a-bitch to move away from my wife!
Burford Do as I say, Mr Drury—or that son-of-a-bitch will take infinite pleasure in slitting your wife's throat.

As Robert hesitates Clayton grabs hold of Stella's hair and forces her head back. The flick-knife is perilously nearer her throat. Robert drops the dagger and moves down to the telephone. Burford puts his notebook near the telephone and points to it

Dial that number . . .

Robert looks at the notebook

When you hear a voice at the other end just read what I've written in that book. If you say anything else on the phone—if you utter one single word more—(*looking across at Clayton*)—you know what will happen.

Robert stares at the notebook, then across at Stella. For a brief moment he hesitates, then he picks up the telephone and dials. A pause—finally a voice is heard at the other end of the line

Robert (*to Burford, staggered*) It's the police!

Burford gives a tense nod, once again indicating the notebook. Clayton tightens his grip on Stella's hair

(*On the telephone, looking at the message in the notebook*) This is Robert Drury speaking . . . Please come at once . . . I've just killed a man . . .!
Burford (*quietly*) Put the phone down!

Robert slowly replaces the telephone

(*To Clayton*) If he makes a move—if he moves one inch—you know what to do! And don't bloody hesitate!

Clayton nods

Burford picks up his notebook and goes quickly out into the hall

Robert stands motionless, angrily staring across at Clayton

Robert If you hurt my wife, you bastard, I'll . . .
Clayton (*tightening his grip even more*) You'll what, Mr Drury?

A pause. The telephone rings. Robert instinctively turns towards the desk

Don't answer it! (*As Robert hesitates*) You heard what I said! Don't answer it!

Robert stares at the telephone, still hesitating. Pause. Clayton looks at Robert as the telephone continues ringing. His manner is tense, threatening, as if he is about to attack Stella with the flick-knife. Robert realizes this and freezes. A long pause—the telephone continues to ring

As the telephone finally stops ringing Burford appears from the hall. He is carrying Crozier's suitcase

Burford (*to Clayton*) Let her go! I've got Crozier's case!

Clayton quickly releases his hold on Stella and joins Burford. Stella immediately slumps forward, obviously suffering from shock

Clayton and Burford go out through the hall

As the men disappear Robert rushes towards Stella

Robert Stella!

Stella begins to shake; she tries desperately to control herself

Stella I can't stop shaking . . .
Robert You will, darling. Just hold on. (*He holds her tight*)
Stella I was so frightened. I really did think he was going to kill me. (*Pause*) Robert, I just can't stop trembling . . .
Robert (*still holding her*) You will, darling . . .

A long pause—during which Stella finally manages to control herself. Robert slowly moves away from her

Stella Who were they? And why did they . . . (*She stops; stares across at the body*) Is he dead?

Robert gives her an anxious look, then moves down to the body. He stands for a moment looking at Crozier, then he kneels down and examines him. Stella makes an effort and joins Robert, her frightened eyes on the dead man. A pause, then—Robert looks at her and, rising, gives a little nod

What's going to happen when the police get here? (*Still staring at the body*) If you tell them about Mike they'll never believe you didn't kill him.
Robert (*softly*) Yes, I know. I realize that.

Stella, worried and still suffering from shock, slowly turns away from him. As she does so the telephone rings. Pause. The telephone continues ringing. Robert hesitates, then crosses to the desk

(*On the telephone*) Hello . . . ? Yes, this is Robert Drury . . . Who is that?

(*To Stella; hand over the mouthpiece*) It's the police! (*On the telephone again, adopting a friendly tone and making a quick decision*) Did I— what . . .? No, I'm afraid I didn't. Why do you ask . . .? (*Apparently astonished*) Are you serious . . .? When did this happen . . .? You were right! It certainly was a hoax. I'm glad you had the sense to ring back . . . I haven't the faintest idea, some young fool trying to be clever, I suppose . . . Not at all, thank *you*, Inspector. (*He replaces the receiver*)

Stella stares at him, taken aback by what she has heard. He moves away from the desk

Stella What's going to happen? What are we going to do?
Robert (*after a moment*) We're going to find Mike!
Stella Find him?
Robert Yes.
Stella But how?

Robert slowly picks up the dagger

Robert That girl knows where Mike is, you heard her say so. When she returns I'm going to make out that I killed Crozier! (*He looks at the dagger*) I'll scare the living daylights out of the bitch!

The Lights fade, as—

The CURTAIN *falls*

SCENE 3

The same. Night

The curtains are drawn and Crozier's body has been taken upstairs. Robert is stretched out in an armchair facing the hall. It is obviously a position he has occupied for some little time. Stella enters from the hall. She is wearing a dressing gown

Robert It's a quarter to eleven. She's late. She said ten o'clock.
Stella I thought I saw her . . .
Robert (*rising, alerted*) You thought you saw her? When?
Stella Just now, coming up the drive. I must have been mistaken . . . (*After a moment; nervously*) You haven't changed your mind?
Robert No, I have not! As soon as she arrives I'm going to take her upstairs and show her Crozier. I've just got to scare the hell out of her, Stella! It's the only way—the only way we have of finding out where Mike is.

A slight pause

Stella Those two men. Burford and—what did the other man call himself?
Robert Clayton.
Stella Who were they, Robert?
Robert (*on edge*) I don't know.

Stella Why did they come here? Was it simply to kill Crozier?

Robert They came for the suitcase. Whether it was their original intention to kill Crozier as well, I wouldn't know. You remember what Crozier said to Vivien Norwood. "Take the case upstairs and *stay with it*." I remember wondering at the time . . .

The doorbell rings

You were right! Here she is! Now leave us—or I won't be able to go through with this!

Stella gives a little nod and goes quickly into the hall

Pause

Robert crosses to the desk and picks up the dagger. He looks at it for a moment, then conceals it behind his back and exits to the hall

Pause. Voices are heard

Dorothy Medway enters, followed by Robert

Dorothy Sorry, barging in like this, I know it's late, but I'm on my way to Kingston and . . . How's Stella? Is she well?

Robert Yes, she's well.

Dorothy I'm staying the night with a girl friend. Got an interview early tomorrow morning.

Robert Yet another interview, Dorothy?

Dorothy (*putting her handbag down*) Yes, and you'll never guess who with. Marks and Spencer. Answered an advertisement. Wrote them a very funny letter. Come to think of it, got a very funny reply. Won't get the job, of course. Never do. Anyway, I didn't come here to talk about myself. I dropped in the cottage this morning just to see if everything was all right and I suddenly noticed that the thingummybob above the bookcase—the scabbard, or dagger, or whatever you call it—was missing.

Robert (*revealing the dagger*) You mean this?

Dorothy Oh, so you've got it! Good! I was quite worried. I thought it had vanished.

Robert Was—anything else missing?

Dorothy No, nothing so far as I could tell. But I knew you set great store by that and I thought . . . Anyway, I'm glad no-one walked off with it.

Robert goes to the bar and Dorothy joins him

Robert (*getting Dorothy a drink*) Was everything all right at the cottage?

Dorothy Absolutely. Oh—Mike's bedroom was in a bit of a mess, which surprised me because I know how fussy Stella is. (*Taking the drink*) Thank you, Robert.

Robert What do you mean, a bit of a mess?

Dorothy You know what kids are. Some of his things were strewn all over the floor. But not to worry, I tidied the place up.

Robert What things? You mean clothes?

Dorothy Yes. His anorak, a T-shirt, some underpants, a couple of pairs of socks which looked to me as if they'd . . .

Robert (*astonished, stopping her*) His anorak and T-shirt were on the floor?

Dorothy (*looking at him*) Yes.

Robert In the bedroom?

Dorothy Yes.

Robert At the cottage?

Dorothy (*amused*) It's the cottage I'm talking about!

Robert What colour was the anorak?

Dorothy (*surprised by Robert's tone*) What colour? Red.

Robert And the T-shirt.

Dorothy What about it?

Robert What did it look like?

Dorothy What did it look like? You must be joking! You've seen it dozens of times.

Robert (*tensely*) What was it like?

Dorothy It was just an ordinary white T-shirt with Mike's name on it. (*Bewildered*) I say, what is this? Has something happened to Mike?

Robert replies after a slight hesitation, ignoring the question

Robert Dorothy, before you go—and I'm afraid you've got to go soon because I'm expecting someone—I'd like you to answer one or two questions.

Dorothy Forgive my saying so, but I think I'm the one who ought to be asking the questions. Not you.

Robert Yes, I know, but you've called at a very awkward time, so please—do as I ask.

A moment's pause

Dorothy All right. Go ahead. What is it you want to know?

Robert This morning, when you visited the cottage—was it empty?

Dorothy Yes.

Robert You didn't see anyone?

Dorothy No, I didn't. (*Puzzled*) Why? Should I have done? Is someone staying there?

Robert No, it's just that . . . You didn't come across anyone? No-one at all?

Dorothy I've just said I didn't.

A slight pause

Robert Did anything unusual happen while you were in the cottage?

Dorothy No, nothing. (*She shrugs*) There was a phone call, a wrong number, but that's all.

Robert A wrong number?

Dorothy Yes, a woman rang up. I thought it was Jane at first, but it wasn't.

Robert What did she say?

Dorothy She just said, "Sorry, I've dialled the wrong number".

Robert What made you think it was Jane?

Dorothy Well—obviously the voice. But it wasn't.
Robert Apart from this morning, when did you last visit the cottage?
Dorothy Three or four days ago.
Robert Was everything all right?
Dorothy Yes, it seemed to be.
Robert Were you alone?
Dorothy Alone? Why do you ask?
Robert Were you, Dorothy?

Dorothy hesitates and drinks before replying

Dorothy Well, no—as a matter of fact I wasn't. I had a friend with me.
Robert Who was this friend?
Dorothy No-one you know.
Robert (*putting the dagger down on the bar*) I've met most of your friends, at some time or other.
Dorothy Yes, well—he's not really a friend, just an acquaintance. His name's Foster. And is he a fan of yours! He must have seen every film you've ever made.
Robert Where did you meet him?
Dorothy He bumped into me—literally bumped into me—in a wine bar about a week ago. He was thrilled to death when he discovered you and I were cousins.
Robert And even more thrilled when you offered to show him the cottage?
Dorothy (*after a pause; avoiding looking at him*) I'm sorry, Robert, I shouldn't have done it, I know—but—I didn't think you'd mind.
Robert Tell me about this man Foster? What does he look like?
Dorothy Oh, dear—I'm not very good at describing people. He's about thirty-eight or nine. Average height. Dark; clean shaven. Bit of a rough diamond, really. (*She puts her drink down and leaves the bar, turning her back on Robert*)
Robert Did he ask you a lot of questions? About me, I mean—and Stella?
Dorothy Well—yes. He was curious. (*Turning*) But then people always are. They never stop asking me questions about you. (*Concerned*) I'm sorry, Robert. I made a mistake. I shouldn't have taken him to the cottage— it won't happen again, I promise you . . . (*She picks up her handbag*)
Robert Have you shown anyone else over the cottage?
Dorothy No, I haven't. (*After a tiny hesitation*) Truly, I haven't.
Robert What about the keys to the cottage? Have you ever lent them to anyone?
Dorothy Good heavens, no! I wouldn't dream of doing a thing like that!
Robert (*dismissing her, not too unfriendly*) All right, Dorothy. Now, if you'll excuse me, I've got someone coming to see me.
Dorothy (*somewhat relieved*) Yes, of course. (*After a moment*) I—I haven't had the cheque this month, Robert.
Robert I know. I overlooked it. Jane's dealing with it.
Dorothy Thank you, my dear.

Dorothy turns towards the hall

Jane enters

She is surprised to see Dorothy whom she quite obviously dislikes

Jane Hello, Dorothy! I didn't know you were here! What are you doing in this part of the world? Don't tell me! Another one of your interviews!
Dorothy That's right.
Jane Selfridges?
Dorothy That was last week. Marks and Spencer.
Jane Well, I'll say one thing, you certainly know how to write persuasive letters.
Dorothy Unfortunately that's only half the battle. Never fail to make an ass of myself when it comes to the interview. If I don't trip up walking into the room I invariably fall flat on my face on the way out. I've still got my Harrods scars. I've been given my marching orders—so I'm off. Say a little prayer to St Michael for me!

Dorothy exits, followed by Robert

Jane moves slowly across the room towards the bar

As Jane reaches the bar, Robert returns

It is difficult to tell whether Jane has noticed the dagger. She certainly gives no obvious indication of having done so

Jane (*turning*) Is there any news?
Robert No, I'm afraid there isn't.
Jane Did you phone your mother?
Robert Yes, but there was no reply.
Jane (*surprised*) No reply?
Robert I'm going to call her in the morning. Jane, forgive me, but Stella's gone to bed and I'm just about to turn in. I've had a pretty tiring day.
Jane Yes, I'm sure you have. I just wondered if you'd heard anything.
Robert No. I'll let you know the moment we have any news.
Jane Please do. (*After a slight hesitation*) I'm very fond of Mike, Robert.
Robert Yes, I know you are.
Jane Tell Stella not to worry, I'm sure everything will be all right.

Jane goes to the desk and picks up a pile of scripts

Robert (*casually*) Oh, by the way. That journalist, Vivien—Norwood, is it?
Jane Yes, Norwood.
Robert Is she a close friend of yours?
Jane No, she's not. In fact, to be honest, I don't really care for Vivien. She's far too opinionated for my liking. But she was most terribly kind to me on one occasion. She really was.
Robert Kind? In what way?

Jane sits on the pouffe

Jane (*laughing*) Oh dear! I was afraid you were going to ask that. Just after Christmas, while you and Stella were in Switzerland, I read a book on Yoga and became absolutely hooked on it.

Robert Yoga? This is news to me.

Jane Yes, I know. At first I just followed the book and did the exercises. Nice, simple, uncomplicated little exercises. Then—heaven only knows why—I joined a class in Richmond. The first couple of days was a wild success. Then on my third day! Ye Gods! My whole body suddenly went rigid. I just couldn't move—not an inch. Fortunately, Vivien, who was in the same class, came to my rescue. Even now I don't know what on earth she did. All I know is—she got me back to the flat and twelve hours later I was out and about.

Robert You were lucky.

Jane You can say that again! Since then we've bumped into each other from time to time, but we've never become what you might call really friendly. (*Indicating the scripts*) I'll pop these in the office. (*She rises*)

Robert Where does she live, do you know?

Jane I haven't the slightest idea. I've never asked her and she's never volunteered the information (*With a sudden thought*) Oh dear! I do hope Stella wasn't annoyed about the interview?

Robert No, no, of course not.

Jane I tried to talk her out of it—Vivien, I mean—but she was very persistent.

Robert Have you met any of her friends?

Jane Very few, come to think of it. Why do you ask?

Robert (*watching for her reaction*) I wondered if she'd ever introduced you to an Italian called Victor Endrico.

Jane Victor Endrico? No, I've never heard of him.

Robert I bumped into him in Rome and I got the impression, I don't know why, that he was a friend of hers.

Jane I wouldn't know.

Robert dismisses her

> *After a momentary hesitation Jane says "Good night" and goes into the office, closing the door behind her*

Robert moves thoughtfully towards the bar. The telephone rings. Robert turns

> *Stella enters from the hall and quickly crosses to the desk*

Stella (*on the telephone; tensely*) Hello? (*A slight pause*) Hello . . .? I'm sorry, I can't hear you . . . (*Puzzled*) Hello . . .?

Robert Who is it?

Stella There doesn't seem to be anyone there. (*On the telephone*) Hello . . .? (*She hesitates, then replaces the receiver*)

Robert (*nodding towards the office*) That was Jane.

Stella Yes, I know, and I thought I heard Dorothy?

Robert You did.

Stella What on earth did Dorothy want?

Robert I forgot to send her the usual cheque, so her visit was a gentle reminder. But apart from that, she called in the cottage this morning and was surprised to find . . .

The telephone rings

It's all right, I'll take it! (*He picks up the telephone*) Hello . . .? Hello? (*He looks at Stella, then speaks on the telephone*) Look, could you please speak up . . .! Hello . . .

Stella Who do you think it is?

Robert I don't know. They're in a call-box. I heard the pips and I could hear the traffic in the background and . . . (*Suddenly, stunned*) Mike!

Stella Mike!

Robert (*incredulously*) . . . Mike, where are you? Where are you speaking from?

Stella (*grabbing his arm*) Is he all right? Is he well? Let me speak to him . . .

Robert (*releasing his arm*) Stella, for God's sake! (*On the telephone*) What's that, Mike . . .? Yes, I'm listening . . . I'm sorry, I can't hear . . . (*He freezes*)

Stella What is it?

Robert (*staring at the receiver*) The bloody phone's gone dead! It's dead! (*He listens*)

Stella Put it down! Replace the receiver!

Robert The phone's dead, I tell you!

Robert continues banging the telephone, then finally—in desperation—he replaces the receiver

Stella Was it Mike? Was it really Mike?

Robert Yes! Oh God . . .

Stella What happened? Were you cut off?

Robert I don't know. He was in a phone box—and you know what those blasted boxes are like!

Stella Try and get the operator . . .

Robert Talk sense! How can I get the operator when the phone . . .

The telephone rings. Robert snatches up the receiver

Hello . . .? Hello, Mike . . .! I—I don't know what happened . . . Yes, I'm listening . . . I'm listening darling . . . Go on . . . Yes, of course . . .! (*To Stella*) Vivien Norwood's with him—she wants to talk to me . . .

Stella How is Mike? Is he crying?

Robert No.

Stella Don't lie to me, Robert!

Robert Stella, please! (*Suddenly, on the telephone again*) Miss Norwood . . . What is it you want? Crozier . . . ? I'm afraid you can't, it's not possible. (*After a moment*) Crozier's dead . . . He was murdered . . . Yes, murdered! Why should I lie to you . . .? I'm telling you the truth . . .! What's that? Two men came, they took Crozier's case . . . I don't know who they were. I'd never seen them before . . . Now put my son on, I want to talk to him! (*Suddenly*) What? (*A long pause; curiously*) Yes, I'm listening . . . Go on . . . Go on, I'm listening . . . (*Another pause; tensely*) Where . . .? Just tell me where . . .! Yes, I know the street, it's

off the Embankment . . . What's that . . . ? (*Looking at Stella*) No-one . . .
Absolutely no-one, I give you my word! Straight away! (*He slams down
the receiver*) She's got Mike and she's handing him over! I'm meeting
the pair of them in Chelsea!

Stella Now? Tonight?

Robert Yes.

Stella But why? Why is she doing this?

Robert She's scared, because of what happened to Crozier. The little bitch
is scared to hell, I could tell by her voice! (*Taking hold of her*) Stella,
listen—she made me promise there'd be no-one with me! Not even you!
She was adamant! (*Stifling a protest from her*) I'll be back with Mike as
quickly as I can!

Robert kisses her and rushes out into the hall

The Lights dim to a Black-out

*The Lights slowly come up. It is nearly two hours later and Stella is anxiously
pacing up and down the room. Somewhere in the background a clock chimes
the hour and she instinctively glances at her watch. There is a very long
pause—during which she lights a cigarette, then, changing her mind,
extinguishes it. She is pacing the room again when there is a tap on the
window. Stella crosses to the window, draws back the curtains, and unlocks
the door*

Vivien enters from the patio

Stella stares at her in amazement

Stella Where's Robert—and Mike? What happened?

Vivien (*puzzled*) What happened?

Stella (*tensely*) Yes—where are they?

Vivien What exactly are you talking about?

Stella You telephoned—you spoke to my husband! You arranged to
meet him!

Vivien I did?

Stella Yes.

Vivien (*quietly, after a moment*) Where did I arrange to meet your husband,
Mrs Drury?

Stella In Chelsea.

Vivien Does Major Crozier know about this? Does he know about the
phone call? (*She moves nearer to Stella*) Where is Crozier? In his room?

*Stella does not answer. Vivien looks at her for a tense moment, then produces
a gun from her bag*

Where is Crozier?

Stella He's dead. He was murdered. Two men came, they said they were
the police. One man was in uniform.

Vivien When? When did they come?

Stella This evening, just after you left . . .

Vivien (*slowly, watching her*) Are you telling me the truth?

Stella Yes, I am!

Vivien What did they look like, these men?
Stella It's—it's difficult to say . . .
Vivien Why is it difficult to say if you saw them? I've got to know what those men looked like! I've got to know who killed Crozier!
Stella One man was about fifty. Bald. He said his name was Burford.
Vivien Burford?
Stella Yes.
Vivien And the other man?
Stella I—I can't remember what the other man looked like . . .
Vivien (*raising the gun, threatening her*) Try to remember!

Stella freezes—but not because of the gun: she has suddenly seen Clayton

Clayton enters from the hall and slowly, cautiously moves towards Vivien

He is still in police uniform and carries a long scarf in his hands

As Vivien finishes speaking, Clayton quickly grabs hold of her, tying the scarf round her neck, and forcing her down on to the pouffe. Stella rushes towards Clayton as he strangles Vivien with the scarf

Stella (*terrified*) No! No!
Clayton Get back!

Burford enters from the hall. He immediately takes control of the situation

Burford No-one's going to hurt you, Mrs Drury.
Stella (*backing away from him as he approaches her*) Who are you? What is it you want?
Burford You're perfectly safe, I assure you. But we thought it advisable to get your husband out of the way whilst we dealt with Miss Norwood. Your husband tends to over-react on these occasions, unlike your son I'm delighted to say, who does precisely what he is told.
Stella (*staring at him*) My son . . . ?
Burford (*smiling*) Yes. Your son. Mike.
Stella (*puzzled*) You know my son. You—know what's happened to him?
Burford Yes, we know. But the situation has changed, Mrs Drury. We now have your son.
Stella You have Mike!
Burford That's right. (*He watches her*)
Stella What—what's going to happen to him?
Burford Nothing. At the moment. Now tell me. Where's Crozier? What did you do with him?

Stella does not answer

Clayton (*picking up Vivien's gun*) You heard what he said! Where's Crozier? Where've you put him?
Stella He's—he's upstairs, in one of the bedrooms.

Burford nods to Clayton, handing him his car keys

Clayton picks up Vivien and carries her out into the hall

Burford What happened after we left here? After you got rid of Crozier? Did anyone contact you? Did any of your friends call?

Stella No, but the police telephoned. They thought Robert's call was a hoax.

Burford goes to the bar and pours himself a drink

Burford Did they? Did they indeed? (*Shaking his head*) It wasn't the police, Mrs Drury. Your husband spoke to a colleague of mine—on both occasions. I was anxious to know whether he'd tell the police the whole story. For your son's sake I was relieved to learn that he wasn't that stupid.

Stella Has Mike been asking for me or his father?

Burford Yes. Yes, of course he has. But tell me, I'm curious. He's also been asking for a Mr UFO. Who's Mr UFO?

Stella Mr UFO?

Burford When I asked Mike if there was anything he particularly wanted, he simply said, "Yes, Mr UFO."

Stella Oh! It's a toy! Jane—our secretary—gave it to him for Christmas.

Burford Well, if it's any consolation to you, it's Mr UFO he's pining for at the moment, not his parents.

A door is heard closing; the sound of voices. Burford turns and looks towards the hall. Robert's voice is heard, raised in anger

Robert (*off, in the hall*) What's going on? Where's my wife? What have you done with my wife?

Robert enters. Clayton is behind him, the gun still in his hand

Stella Robert!

Burford (*pleasantly*) Good evening, Mr Drury.

Robert (*to Burford*) What are you doing here? Why the hell have you come back? Were you responsible for that phone call? For getting me out of the house? (*He goes to Stella*)

Burford I'm sorry you had a wasted journey. I know exactly how you feel.

Robert I doubt it! I doubt very much if you know how I feel! (*Taking hold of Stella*) Darling, are you all right?

Stella gives a little nod

Burford No one's touched your wife, Mr Drury. But I would like to talk to you about your son.

Clayton picks up Vivien's bag and exits

Robert (*to Burford angrily*) My son! What about my son?

Burford (*friendly, a shade patronizingly*) It's always frustrating waiting for someone to turn up, but do try and relax. I suggest you get yourself a large whisky and soda.

Robert (*even angrier than before*) And I suggest, if you've got anything to say, then say it!

Burford stares at Robert, then he puts down his glass and slowly turns towards Stella

Burford As you already know, Mrs Drury, we have your son. How we rescued him from Crozier—if "rescue" is the right word—I don't propose to tell you. But one thing I will tell you, because it's important—something you ought to know. Both of you. (*After a moment, to Robert*) Your son's safety, his very life in fact, is dependent on one factor, and one factor only. Your willingness to co-operate with me.

Stella gives Robert a look; it is obvious that Burford's quiet threat has frightened her

Robert (*making a determined effort to control his true feelings*) My wife and I only have the one child. We're devoted to him.
Stella We'll do anything, anything in the world to get him back.
Robert So will you please tell us what it is you want!
Burford (*friendly again*) I'll be delighted to tell you. In fact, that's why I'm here!
Robert Then what is it? Money?
Burford No, it's not money.
Robert Then what do you want, for God's sake!

Burford picks up his glass again and drinks. After a moment he lowers the glass and looks at Robert

Burford I want to stay here, in this house, for the next forty-eight hours. That is—tonight and tomorrow night. Then, if everything is satisfactory, I shall take leave of you on Friday afternoon.
Robert But that's what Crozier wanted!
Burford That's right, Mr Drury. (*He finishes his drink*)

CURTAIN

ACT II

Scene 1

The same. The action continues where the previous Act stopped

Robert But that's what Crozier wanted!

Burford That's right, Mr Drury. (*He finishes his drink*) You have my word that your son will be released the moment I leave this house, provided of course you have the good sense to do exactly what I tell you. (*He moves to the bar and puts down his glass*) Sometime within the next half-hour, perhaps even sooner, you'll receive another visitor. His name is Henderson. Philip Henderson. He's a friend—or was a friend—of Major Crozier's.

Stella Is that why he's coming here, to meet Major Crozier?

Burford smiles at Stella and gives a little nod. Stella looks at Robert, puzzled

Robert But Crozier's dead.

Burford Yes. Which means that I shall be entertaining Mr Henderson, and not Major Crozier.

Robert Is that why Crozier came here in the first place, to wait for this man? Is that why you're here?

Burford That's right, Mr Drury. (*To Stella*) I'd like you to be particularly nice to Henderson. Please go out of your way to be pleasant to him. (*Turning to Robert*) Now tell me a little about your secretary. Miss Mercer. Does she live with you?

Robert No, she has a flat in Weybridge.

Burford And she reports for work every morning?

Robert Yes.

Burford At what time?

Robert It varies. Ten—quarter-past.

Burford How long does she stay?

Robert Until about six. (*Watching Burford's reaction*) But surely, you don't need me to tell you about my secretary? You must know all there is to know about her by now.

Burford (*apparently puzzled by Robert's remark*) Why do you say that?

Robert It was Jane—Miss Mercer—that brought Vivien Norwood to the house.

Burford Norwood was working for Crozier, not me. I've never met Miss Mercer and I've no wish to do so. Phone her first thing tomorrow morning and tell her she can have the rest of the week off.

Robert Considering that you've never met my secretary you seem to

know a great deal about us. Who told you about our cottage? Was it
your friend Foster, by any chance?
Burford Foster? (*To Stella, with slightly forced amusement*) Who on earth
is Foster?

Clayton enters. He is no longer in police uniform

Robert looks at him, then at Burford

Clayton (*to Burford*) I want a word with you.
Burford Is it important?
Clayton Could be.

Burford hesitates, his eyes on Robert, then he exits with Clayton

Stella What was that about the cottage and someone called Foster?
Robert A man calling himself Foster got friendly with Dorothy. I'm
pretty sure it was Clayton. He quizzed her about us and eventually
conned her into showing him the cottage. This morning Dorothy found
Mike's anorak and T-shirt, they were on the floor in the bedroom.
Stella At the cottage?
Robert Yes. It's my opinion they were planted there to convey the impression that, at some point, Mike was taken to the cottage—and is
probably still in Dorset somewhere.
Stella And you don't think he is? You don't think they did take him to
the cottage!
Robert No, I don't. I have a feeling the clothes were simply a ploy. It's
my bet the poor kid's not far from here, probably in London some
place.
Stella In London?
Robert Yes. It's just a hunch, but ... (*He looks towards the hall; he is
distinctly on edge*) Stella, there's something I've got to tell you! Something important! Tonight—when Mike didn't turn up, when I finally
realized that he wasn't going to appear I—telephoned McKenna.
Stella McKenna! You mean—you sent for the police?
Robert Yes.
Stella (*aghast*) My God, if Burford finds out what you've done!
Robert I had no choice. I was desperate. (*Taking hold of her*) Now, please
—listen to me! I met McKenna and a colleague of his, I told them the
whole story. McKenna's friend—a man from the Special Branch—gave
me this. (*He produces a tiny device from his pocket*)
Stella What is it?
Robert It's a device. An electronic device. McKenna said if we can get it
to Mike without Burford knowing there's a chance, an outside chance,
that the police will be able to locate him.
Stella But how on earth can we get it to him?
Robert When Burford comes back I want you to ask him to let you see
Mike ...
Stella It won't have the slightest effect.
Robert It might; it just might. Plead with him. Beg him to let you see Mike.
Really go to town on him, Stella.

Stella All right, I'll try. But even if he agrees, how could I get that to him?

Robert (*looking at the device*) I don't know. We'll just have to hide it in something.

Stella Clothes! I could take him some clean clothes . . .

Robert No. They'd search the clothes . . .

Stella Well, there must be something else he needs. (*Suddenly*) He's been asking for a toy.

Robert looks at her

Robert A toy? What toy?

Stella Mr UFO. The one Jane gave him for Christmas.

Robert How do you know he's been asking for it?

Stella Burford told me.

Robert (*thoughtfully*) I know the toy you mean—I mended it for him, just before we left on our trip. Where is the toy now?

Stella It's upstairs. In Mike's room.

Robert looks at the device he is holding

Robert It's perfect!

Stella stares at him, realizing what he is thinking. Suddenly they both hear a noise in the hall and Robert quickly puts the device back in his pocket

Burford enters

Burford Clayton tells me there's a room on the second floor which is locked.

Robert Yes, there is.

Burford Why is it locked? None of the other bedrooms are.

Robert We use it as a store room. We keep our ski things in it.

Burford Is there a phone in the room?

Robert No, there isn't.

Burford Where does it look on to?

Robert The drive and a corner of the summer house.

Burford I'd like to take a look at it.

Robert My wife isn't very well. I don't want to leave her, not at the moment.

Burford looks across at Stella. After a pause Stella turns and faces him

Stella Please may I see Mike? Just for a moment—even if I'm not allowed to talk to him. Please just let me see his face. Just so I know he's all right. Please, Mr Burford, I won't be any trouble.

There is a long pause. Burford appears impassive. Then suddenly, to Stella's surprise, he gives a little smile

Burford I'm sorry, Mrs Drury, I know how you feel and I'd like to do what you suggest. But it's not possible. I know only too well what would happen the moment you set eyes on your son. You'd break down, probably become hysterical, and the end result would simply be that the boy would refuse to co-operate with us any longer. It's just not on, I'm afraid.

Stella is about to continue her plea. Burford stops her

However, I'll tell you what I will do. To reassure you, to put your mind completely at rest, I'll let your husband see Mike. (*Turning to Robert*) If that's agreeable to you, I'll tell Clayton and the pair of you can leave almost immediately. But first, perhaps you'll be good enough to show me that room.

Burford turns and goes out. Robert is taken aback by Burford's offer. He stares at Stella, who is equally surprised, then he slowly follows Burford out into the hall

Stella watches him go then moves to the bar. She picks up a packet of cigarettes, then pauses—her thoughts still on Burford's unexpected proposal. She is about to open the packet when she hears a noise. She puts the cigarettes down and with a puzzled look crosses towards the office

The office door suddenly opens and Jane appears

Stella Why, Jane! What are you doing here?
Jane (*urgently*) Stella, I've got to talk to you!
Stella (*with a frightened look towards the hall*) Not now—not now—I'm sorry . . .
Jane (*astonished*) But I've got something to tell you! It's important!
Stella (*her eyes still on the hall*) Jane, please! We can't talk. Not tonight!

Stella closes the hall door, then quickly goes and draws the window curtains

Jane Why can't we talk? What's happening? (*Looking past Stella in the direction of the hall*) Are you in some kind of trouble? Is someone here?
Stella Jane, do as I tell you! Please go!
Jane (*surprised by Stella's tone*) All right, if that's what you want! But first, there's something I've got to tell you. It's about Robert.
Stella (*looking at her*) About Robert?
Jane Yes.
Stella What—what about him?
Jane (*after a moment*) He didn't tell you the truth this afternoon. I telephoned his mother. I asked her how Mike was. The poor woman was bewildered, utterly bewildered. She hadn't the slightest idea what I was talking about.
Stella (*tensely, yet relieved*) Yes. Yes, I know. Mike's not ill.
Jane Then what's happened to him? Where is he?
Stella I'm sorry, Jane. I can't tell you. I mustn't tell you.
Jane Why not? I'm devoted to Mike. I always have been, you know that.

Stella nods

Don't you trust me, Stella?
Stella Yes, of course I trust you. But you must trust me too. Now please do as I say—and go!

Jane All right. (*She moves towards the office, then hesitates*) Stella, has Vivien Norwood got anything to do with this? Robert kept asking me about her.

Stella No, no, of course not.

Jane I hope you mean that, because if she has, I feel responsible.

Stella Yes, of course I mean it. She has nothing to do with it.

Jane looks at Stella, a little bewildered

Jane Stella, forgive me, but—I don't think you're telling me the truth. Something has happened to Mike, and I've a right to know what it is!

Stella (*a note of desperation in her voice*) Jane, I'm sorry, but—if you don't leave this house immediately, you'll have no further rights here at all!

Jane (*taken aback*) Very well.

Jane exits into the office

Stella returns to the bar and thoughtfully picks up the packet of cigarettes again. She reaches for a lighter

Clayton enters from the hall. He is surprised to find Stella alone and quickly joins her

Stella instinctively tries to move away from the bar but Clayton blocks her exit. He stands looking at her, an impudent smile on his face

Clayton What's the hurry?

Stella Please put your arm down, I want to pass.

Clayton And I want a drink, Mrs Drury . . .

Stella Then get one . . .

Clayton I'd rather you get it for me.

There is a pause. Stella faces him, defiantly

Stella Will you please do as I say and let me pass!

Clayton (*taking hold of her*) You know, you and I are going to see quite a bit of each other. So don't be bloody-minded. Now get me a drink. (*He releases his hold on her and sits at the bar*)

Stella hesitates, then returns to the bar

Scotch—or vodka—I'm easy either way.

Stella picks up a glass and a bottle of Scotch. She pours the drink. Clayton takes the glass

(*Over-politely, eyeing her neckline with interest*) Thank you. That's very kind of you. I appreciate it. Skol! (*He drinks. Pause. Still staring at her, and admiring what he sees*) It's not difficult to see who that son of yours takes after. He's a good-looking kid. Got guts too.

Stella Where is Mike? Where have you taken him?

Clayton laughs

Clayton Come on! You don't expect me to answer that question, now do you? (*He looks at his drink; quickly finishes it and hands her the glass*) Very nice. Now make it a real drink this time.

Stella stares at him for a moment, then picks up the bottle of Scotch and fills his glass to the brim

(*Irritated*) Don't be a silly bitch!

Stella You said you wanted a large one.

Clayton (*taking the drink from her*) Yes, well—I've got news for you, Stella. It is Stella, isn't it? I don't talk when I get pissed. It just turns me on. (*He starts to drink*)

Burford enters. He is carrying a strip of dark cloth; to be used as a blindfold. He stands looking at Clayton, obviously displeased by what he sees

Clayton suddenly realizes that he is being watched and swings round on his stool

I'm having a drink. I reckon I've earned one.

Burford (*ignoring him*) Mrs Drury . . .

Stella Yes?

Stella comes from behind the bar and joins Burford

Burford I've given your husband permission to take Mike the toy he's been asking for, together with a box of pencils.

Stella (*softly*) Thank you.

Burford He's also trying to find some drawing paper. Perhaps you can help him.

Stella (*nodding*) There's some in the office.

Stella goes into the office

Burford goes to Clayton who drinks, then slowly puts his glass down

Burford (*with a nod towards the office*) Don't get any wild ideas. This is a once in a lifetime operation. I don't want it buggered up. (*As he finishes speaking he moves behind Clayton and viciously grabs hold of his hair*)

Clayton Surely I'm entitled to a drink when I feel like one! And don't kid yourself, the success of this operation doesn't depend on me, or you either, come to that!

Burford No?

Clayton No! We're in Henderson's hands—or will be, *if* he turns up!

Burford He'll turn up and when he does you know what to do.

Clayton All right, but I still have my doubts about him. We still don't know whether he'll play.

Burford (*angrily letting go of Clayton's head*) I'll handle Henderson! Leave Henderson to me! (*A brief pause*) Now remember what I told you about Drury. Let him see the boy—just for three or four minutes. No longer. Then you blindfold him again, bring him back here, and lock him in the summer house. I gave you the key.

Clayton nods

You'll find a rope on one of the chairs. Tie him up, gag him, and tighten the blindfold. And be sure to make a good job of it. Whatever happens he mustn't have a clue as to where he is.

Clayton Why does he have to see the boy at all?

Burford When this episode is over, Drury and I will have a little chat about expenses. So it'll be to our advantage if he's convinced that the boy is alive and well.

Clayton nods and reaches for his drink. Burford forestalls him and, picking up the glass, empties the whisky into a martini jug which is on the bar

Clayton What the hell!

Burford Use your head! You don't want an accident, not with Drury in the car.

Robert enters from the hall. He is holding a pencil box of crayons and the space toy—Mr UFO

Robert Where's my wife?

Burford She's looking for some drawing paper. She'll be back in a moment. (*He indicates the sofa*) Sit down, Mr Drury.

Robert hesitates, then moves towards the sofa. He does not sit. Clayton takes a length of cord out of his pocket and moves down to Robert

Robert What's that for?

Clayton Wrists.

Robert Oh my God . . .

Burford (*to Clayton for Robert's benefit*) There's no need for that.

Clayton I think there is.

Burford Put it away.

Clayton I'm taking no chances. If I don't tie him—we don't go!

Burford looks at Robert

Burford I'm sorry, you can see his point. It's quite a long journey and you'll be in the back of the car. (*To Clayton*) Okay—but you remove the blindfold the minute he enters the building. You understand?

Clayton If that's what you want.

Burford That's what I want. Under no circumstances must the boy see the blindfold. You can replace it later, when you're leaving.

Clayton nods and moves nearer to Robert. He makes a gesture, indicating that he wants Robert to hold out his hands. Robert hesitates then, putting down the toy and the pencil box, he offers Clayton his wrists. Clayton binds Robert's wrists with the cord

Stella enters from the office carrying a large drawing book

Stella Here's a drawing book for Mike. (*She stops, stares at Robert's wrists, then at Burford*) What's that for? What on earth are you doing that for?

Burford I'm afraid it's necessary, Mrs Drury—and the blindfold. Just for the journey.

Robert It's all right, darling. It doesn't make the slightest difference.

Burford hands Clayton the cloth and points to the sofa. He then picks up the toy together with the pencil box. He looks at the toy, obviously intrigued by it. Robert glances at him, anxiously, then looks away again. Stella's eyes are on Burford

Burford (*amused*) So this is Mr UFO. Does he work?
Robert Sometimes . . .

A tiny pause

Burford (*after looking at the toy again*) I'll put these in the car.

   Burford exits

Robert gives Stella a tiny smile then sits on the sofa. Clayton goes behind the sofa and proceeds to blindfold him. Pause. Clayton crosses to Stella and takes the drawing book from her

Clayton (*to Robert*) Let's go!
Stella Give my love to Mike.

Clayton returns to the sofa, takes hold of Robert's arm, and leads him towards the hall. Stella makes a move, as if about to say something else, then stops

   Robert exits with Clayton

Stella gives a sigh of relief and sinks down on to the pouffe. She buries her head in her hands, trying desperately to recover from the tension of the last few minutes

   Burford returns. He is carrying Mr UFO

Stella realizes that he has returned but she does not immediately look up

Burford If I were you I'd go to bed, Mrs Drury.
Stella I'd rather stay here.
Burford It'll be some considerable time before your husband returns.
Stella I'm aware of that . . . (*She looks up and sees Mr UFO. She rises, staring at the toy in amazement*)
Burford Oh—I changed my mind about Mr UFO. Your husband seemed rather too interested in it. (*He smiles and puts the toy down on the sofa*) Take my advice and go to your room, Mrs Drury. You've got a very long wait ahead of you. (*As Stella hesitates*) There's not the slightest point in your staying here. Besides Henderson is due any minute and I'd prefer you were not here when he arrives.
Stella Why?
Burford You'll meet Henderson later. Now, please—do as I say.
Stella Very well. But first—will you tell me something? Why didn't you let me see Mike, instead of Robert? (*A pause*) Was it simply because I might get emotional and make things difficult for you?
Burford Yes.

Stella No other reason?

Burford What other reason could there be?

Stella It occurred to me that you might have wanted my husband out of the way again.

Burford I'm afraid your imagination is playing you tricks, Mrs Drury. Now go to your room. I'll let you know the moment your husband gets back.

Stella hesitates, then finally exits

Burford picks up the toy and moves to the desk. He carefully examines Mr UFO, then sits in the chair and searches for a letter opener. He finds the letter opener and is about to use it, in an attempt to take the toy apart, when the doorbell rings

> *Burford puts Mr UFO on the desk, looks quickly around the room, then goes out into the hall*

Pause. There is the sound of men's voices. Another pause

> *A Man enters. In spite of the fact that his clothes are different from Robert's, he looks like Robert, he moves like Robert. He is Robert Drury's look-alike. It is only when he speaks that we notice a slight difference*

The Man looks slowly around the room, obviously interested in his surroundings. There is a long pause

> *Burford enters*

(*Pleasantly*) I've taken your case upstairs, Mr Henderson. Now— would you care for a drink before I show you to your room? I expect you could do with one.

Henderson (*turning, a note of suspicion in his voice*) You say Crozier's not here?

Burford I'm afraid not. He's in Paris.

Henderson Paris? What the devil is he doing in Paris? He arranged to meet me here, tonight!

Burford Yes, I know. I'm aware of the arrangements you made with Major Crozier.

Henderson (*coldly*) Are you? Are you indeed? Then perhaps you'll tell me who you are—and what you're doing here?

Burford Certainly. But first—let me get you your drink.

Henderson (*as Burford moves towards the bar*) We'll skip the drink, Mr— Burford did you say your name was?

Burford (*turning, quietly*) Yes. Burford.

Henderson We'll skip the drink, Mr Burford.

Burford Very well. As you please. (*A brief pause*) I'm a close friend and confidant—a partner in fact—of Major Crozier's.

Henderson I didn't know Crozier had a partner—or any friends either, if it comes to that.

Burford Well—he has, I assure you. And, in case you're interested, I'm a very active partner, Mr Henderson.

The two men take each other in. Burford just managing to conceal the fact that he finds Henderson a shade too arrogant for his liking

Henderson If Crozier's not here, where are Mr and Mrs Drury?

Burford Mr and Mrs Drury?

Henderson Yes. Why aren't they here to welcome me? They invited me. I'm their guest.

Burford (*taken aback*) They invited you?

Henderson Yes, of course!

Burford (*slowly, staring at him*) I find that somewhat difficult to believe . . .

Henderson Do you? Then obviously you're not very well informed after all. But you still haven't answered my question. Where are they?

Burford Robert Drury had a meeting in London, it went on longer than he expected so he's staying the night. Mrs Drury wasn't feeling well. You'll make her acquaintance in the morning.

Henderson I see.

Burford (*affably*) Mr Henderson, as I understand it, you first met Major Crozier about a month ago, in Monte Carlo.

Henderson That's right. We bumped into each other in the casino.

Burford What happened?

Henderson What happened? I lost rather a lot of money.

Burford And later? What happened later?

Henderson Crozier was kind enough to help me out.

Burford (*smiling*) And presumably, at some point, you bumped into each other again?

Henderson On several occasions. But what exactly are you getting at? What is it you want to know?

Burford I'd like to know what Crozier said to you.

Henderson Then I suggest you ask Crozier.

Burford (*pleasantly*) I'm asking you, Mr Henderson.

Henderson hesitates. He looks at Burford, undecided whether to satisfy his curiosity or not

Henderson (*finally*) Crozier made out he was a personal friend of Robert Drury's and that Drury was anxious to meet me. He said that Drury had an idea for a film—based on the fact that I was his double—and that if I was prepared to co-operate I couldn't fail to make less than a hundred thousand dollars out of the deal . . .

Burford Go on.

Henderson Some time later I had a phone call from Crozier saying that he'd received an invitation to stay with Mr and Mrs Drury and that I'd also been invited.

Burford And you believed that?

Henderson Of course I believed it! Why shouldn't I?

Burford You actually believed that ridiculous story? (*Amused*) You've been conned, my friend!

Henderson (*angrily*) What d'you mean, conned!

Burford Well and truly conned! (*With great finality*) There is no film deal in the offing and never, at any time, did Robert Drury express a wish to meet you.

Henderson Then what the hell was Crozier playing at?

Burford Before I answer that question there's something I've got to know ...

Henderson About what?

Burford About you, Mr Henderson. Is it true that you once worked in Hatton Garden and were considered something of an expert in diamonds?

Henderson (*nodding*) Yes. But that was some time ago. I'll send you a copy of my autobiography when I get down to writing it. Now perhaps you'll satisfy *my* curiosity. Why am I here? What exactly is it you and Crozier want from me?

A significant pause

Burford We want you to fly to New York under the name of Robert Drury. You'll have Robert Drury's passport and you'll be accompanied by his wife.

Henderson Accompanied by his wife?

Burford That's right.

Henderson (*puzzled*) I don't understand. I don't get this.

Burford I think you do. We're asking you to be Robert Drury—from the moment you leave this house until you clear the customs at Heathrow and Kennedy Airport.

Henderson Does Mrs Drury know about this?

Burford Not yet. But don't you worry about Mrs Drury. She'll do precisely what I want her to do.

Pause

Henderson And what happens when we reach New York?

Burford You both check in the Waldorf Astoria hotel. You then take a cab, alone, to an address on East Forty-seventh Street.

Henderson And what do I deliver to this address on East Forty-seventh Street?

Burford You see, you do understand the situation after all. You understand it perfectly. You'll deliver a suitcase to a man called Steve Kirchner. He will produce a valise containing a large number of diamonds. You examine the diamonds, and only when you are one hundred per cent satisfied that the stones are genuine, will you hand over the suitcase in exchange for the diamonds.

Henderson And then what happens?

Burford You rejoin Mrs Drury at the Waldorf Astoria, entertain her for dinner, and the following morning you both fly back to London.

Henderson With the diamonds, no doubt?

Burford With the diamonds. I have a client, a gentleman from the Middle East, who can't wait to get his hands on them.

Henderson And what happens if the customs get their hands on me?

Burford That's a risk you've got to take. But don't forget you'll be Robert Drury. You'll get full V.I.P. treatment, both ways—with Mrs Drury as cover.

Henderson (*giving the matter thought*) What makes you think Mrs Drury will go along with this?

Burford The fact that—the fact that she has no alternative.

Pause

Henderson It's an interesting proposition, but there's two things you haven't told me. One: what's in the case . . .

Burford Nothing of importance, as far as you're concerned.

Henderson Really? And for delivering this case which contains nothing of importance—I get what?

Burford (*after a moment*) You get what Crozier said you'd get—a hundred thousand dollars.

Henderson When?

Burford When?

Henderson When do I get the hundred thousand dollars?

Burford You get twenty thousand on the way to Heathrow. The rest on your return to London. (*Pause*) Well—Mr Henderson? What do you say?

Another pause

Henderson I'll sleep on it.

Burford (*surprised and none too pleased*) I'm sorry, that won't do. We must have your decision now. Tonight!

Henderson stares at Burford for a long moment

Henderson I've given you my decision. I'll sleep on it. Now perhaps you'll be good enough to show me to my room . . .

Henderson moves towards the hall as the Lights fade and—

the CURTAIN *falls*

SCENE 2

The same. A few hours later

Clayton rushes into the room and makes straight for the bar. He looks angry and agitated as he quickly pours himself a drink. There is blood and an ugly cut down one side of his face. Burford enters and stands watching him. Clayton downs the drink in one quick gulp and immediately proceeds to pour himself another one

Clayton Has Henderson arrived?

Burford (*staring at Clayton's face*) Yes. We'll talk about Henderson later. You still haven't told me what happened!

Clayton (*angrily*) What happened? (*Indicating his face*) This bloody happened!

Burford Did Drury do that?

Clayton He did! The little shit!

Burford (*sharply*) Where is Drury?

Clayton Where do you think he is? He's in the summer house!

Burford Tell me about it.

Clayton stares at him; does not answer

I've got to know sooner or later.

A slight pause

Clayton I did what you told me. Drove straight to the bungalow. He was quiet, no trouble, not a squeak out of him—not even when he saw the boy. Then on the way back, I don't know why, I began to feel uneasy.

Burford Go on . . .

Clayton We got to the summer house. I unlocked the door and told him to get inside. He just nodded and did as he was told. Then, as I lent over to get the rope—the bastard swung round and hit me.

Burford Then what happened?

Clayton What d'you think! I put the boot in and bloody quick, I can tell you!

Burford Let's hear the rest.

Clayton That's it. There's no more.

Burford Where did you leave him?

Clayton I've told you. In the summer house.

Burford On the floor?

Clayton Yes.

Burford Was he conscious?

Clayton You must be joking!

Burford angrily grabs hold of Clayton, pulling him across the room, and forcing him down on to the pouffe

Burford (*twisting Clayton's arm*) Did you gag him? Did you gag him and use the rope like I told you?

Clayton (*in pain*) Of course I did! He's safe, I tell you! My arm! My God, my arm!

Burford Give me the key! The key!

Clayton hands him the key

What did you say to upset him?

Clayton I just made a crack about his wife, that's all.

Burford You stupid sod!

Burford rushes out into the hall

Clayton slowly rises and crosses to the bar. He stands for a moment rubbing his arm, then he pours himself a drink

Stella enters

They stare at each other for a moment, then Clayton puts the glass down and comes from behind the bar

Stella Where's my husband?

Clayton He stayed with the boy. He'll be back later.

Stella Is—is Mike ill?

Clayton No. No, he's fine. He's in very good shape. Better than yours truly, I'm afraid.

Stella (*frightened and a little suspicious*) What have you done to your face?

Clayton Now that's a very good question. Nice of you to ask. (*Moving towards her*) Would you like to hear about it?

Stella (*receding*) No, I wouldn't . . . (*Glancing towards the hall*) I want to speak to Burford.

Clayton And so you shall. So you shall! But first, I think it would be a good idea if you listened to what I have to say!

As Clayton finishes speaking Stella makes a sudden movement towards the hall. Clayton forestalls her. They stand for a moment looking at each other, then in a display of fury he seizes hold of her arm

Stella Leave go! Please leave go of me!

Stella struggles, finally breaking away and backing towards the bar. Clayton produces a gun, intent on striking her with it

Clayton Now I'll tell you what happened to this face of mine since you're interested! That husband of yours hit me! Take a good look at it! Because you're now going to pay for what that little shit did!

Stella faces him, terrified, her right hand groping wildly across the bar. She suddenly finds Clayton's drink, grasps the glass, and tosses the Scotch straight into his face. With a cry of anguish Clayton covers his face with his hands. He staggers blindly back from the bar

Stella Get out! Leave me! Leave me alone!

Clayton cries, whimpering with pain as he feels the cut on his face. Finally, he rushes out into the hall

Stella moves away from the bar. She is trembling now and on the verge of tears. She moves to the sofa

(*Softly*) Robert . . . Oh, my God, Robert! (*She sinks on to the arm of the sofa and stays there for a little while, trying desperately to gain control of herself. Finally she stops the tears, rises, and begins searching her pockets for a handkerchief*)

As Stella finds the handkerchief Henderson enters

Stella (*with a cry of astonishment, starting forward*) Robert! (*She stops, utterly bewildered*) You're—you're not Robert! (*Staring at him*) Who are you?

Henderson My name is Henderson, Mrs Drury. Philip Henderson.

Stella Henderson? You're the man Burford mentioned!

Henderson That's right.

Stella What are you doing here? What is it you want?

Henderson I was under the impression that I'd been invited here. That your husband wanted to discuss some sort of a film deal with me. I realize now that isn't true. (*With a glance towards the bar*) Please forgive me—but may I help myself to a drink? I really need one at the moment.

Stella gives a tense little nod and, still somewhat taken aback by Henderson's appearance, watches him as he crosses to the bar and helps himself to a large Scotch and soda

Stella You're—you're so like Robert! People must constantly mistake you for him.

Henderson It happens all the time. I try very hard not to take advantage of it. But that isn't always possible. (*Looking at her*) Like tonight, for instance.

Stella Tonight?

Henderson Crozier and his partner want me to impersonate your husband. They've offered to make it worth my while. And since I'm in debt to the tune of . . .

Stella (*stopping him*) Crozier, did you say?

Henderson Yes.

Stella But Crozier's dead!

Henderson (*taken aback*) Dead?

Stella Yes.

Henderson moves down to her

Henderson Surely you're mistaken. He's in Paris.

Stella Who told you that? Burford?

Henderson Yes.

Stella Crozier's dead. He was murdered by Burford. I saw it happen, so did my husband. If you don't believe me go upstairs. You'll find his body in one of the bedrooms.

Henderson (*visibly shaken*) Tell me about this man Burford. What do you know about him?

Stella We don't know anything about him except that he's kidnapped our son—Mike. When he first arrived here he pretended he was a police officer. There was another man with him, a man called Clayton.

Henderson You say Burford's kidnapped your son?

Stella Yes, and the extraordinary thing is, we don't really know why he's done it.

Henderson Where is your husband now, Mrs Drury?

Stella Burford agreed that he could see Mike and he left here some time ago with Clayton. Clayton's returned but there's no sign of Robert.

Henderson You've no idea where they've taken him?

Stella No, I haven't.

Henderson gives a little nod and turns away from Stella. He appears thoughtful as he finishes his drink and puts down the glass

Henderson I think I know what's happened to your husband, Mrs Drury. He's been abducted.

Stella By Burford? But why would he do that when he's already got Mike?

Henderson He wants your husband out of the way—out of circulation—during the next forty-eight hours. By then, if everything goes according to plan—Burford's plan, that is—you and I will be on our way to New York.

Stella (*staring at him*) New York? You and I?

Henderson Burford wants me to impersonate your husband, deliver a case to a man called Steve Kirchner and bring back a valise containing diamonds—stolen diamonds, I imagine.

Stella Did he tell you what was in the case?

Henderson No, but since he's prepared to pay me a fair amount of money it's obviously something the Customs people mustn't get their hands on.

Stella And you've agreed to do this?

Henderson No. I said I'd sleep on it. But in view of what you've told me about Mr Burford, I hardly think sleep is on the agenda at the moment.

Stella I've told you the truth.

Henderson Yes—I believe you have, Mrs Drury. I do believe you have!

Stella Then—what are you going to do?

Henderson I don't know. I'm not sure. I'm tempted by Burford's offer because, believe me, I need money right now—a great deal of money. And I'd get away with the impersonation, I'm sure of that. (*Impersonating Robert*) "So you want my autograph my dear. What's your name, young lady?"

Stella gives a little smile

Stella Supposing you decide to go ahead with this—supposing we both do what Burford wants . . .

Henderson looks at her

What do you think will happen to my son?

Henderson I imagine he'll be released when we return to London.

Stella Do you really think that? Do you really think that's what Burford has in mind? (*Pause*) And what happens if the plan fails—if you're caught?

Henderson I don't know. I've been trying to imagine what would happen under those circumstances. I guess I'd just have to try and talk my way out of things. Tell the Customs people the whole story. It wouldn't be the first time I've talked my way out of a tight situation.

Stella And then what would happen to Mike, to say nothing of my husband? (*With a desperate shake of the head, her voice breaking slightly*) It's not on! It's completely out of the question so far as I'm concerned!

Henderson makes no comment. There is a long, sympathetic silence during which he is quietly studying Stella

Henderson Mrs Drury, I have a proposition to put to you. It occurred to me just now when you told me about your boy. (*After a momentary hesitation*) If I can persuade Burford to release your son would you be prepared to give me—lend me, that is—fifty thousand pounds?

Stella stares at him for a moment

Stella (*with peculiar intensity*) Yes, I would.

Henderson Are you sure? Can you lay your hands on that amount of cash?

Stella Yes, I can.

Henderson When?

Stella As soon as the banks open. But what makes you think you can talk Burford into releasing Mike?

Henderson Burford needs me. Without me he can't operate. I'm the lynch-pin. I'll do everything I possibly can to help you. I promise. Just you leave Burford to me, Mrs Drury.

Henderson exits

Stella moves down to the desk. She stands by the desk for some little time, turning over in her mind the information she has received from Henderson. As she finally moves away from the desk the telephone rings. She turns and quickly answers it

Stella (*on the telephone*) Hello ... Yes, this is Weybridge nine-eight-seven-three ... Hello ...? Who is that ...? (*Suddenly recognizing the voice*) Oh, hello, Mother ...! I'm sorry, darling, I can't hear you ... It's a dreadful line ... Mike ...? What—what about Mike? No, no, he's perfectly all right ... Yes, I know Jane phoned you, she told me ... There's nothing for you to worry about, my dear ... Really, Mother ... Jane misunderstood something I said, that's all ... I'm sorry, Robert isn't here at the moment ... No, don't do that I'll get him to ring you ... Yes, of course I will ... And you take care of yourself. (*She replaces the receiver*)

Burford enters

Burford Who was that on the phone?

Stella It was my mother-in-law. She wanted to speak to Robert.

Burford Your mother-in-law? Where is she? Where was she speaking from?

Stella She lives in Italy, near Florence. She was worried about her grandson. She thought he was ill.

Burford Why should she think that?

Stella That's the story we told Jane—our secretary. Jane telephoned Robert's mother; the poor woman was bewildered.

Burford I hope you're telling me the truth, Mrs Drury. (*He stares at her for a moment; decides to believe her story*) Your husband's been very stupid. He attacked Clayton. He should try to control that temper of his. If he doesn't ...

Stella (*stopping him*) Where is Robert? What have you done with him?

Burford We've locked him in the summer house and if he tries to escape he knows only too well what will happen—to the boy. Now sit down. There's something I've got to discuss with you. Something important.

Stella I don't want to sit down—and I refuse to discuss anything until you release my husband. And that, Mr Burford, includes Henderson and your plans for New York!

Burford (*surprised*) You've seen Henderson?

Stella Yes, I've seen him. He came down to get a drink.

Burford How much did he tell you?

Stella I won't discuss Henderson, I won't discuss anything—not until I've seen Robert!

Burford (*losing his temper*) What else did he tell you! I want to know! (*He moves angrily towards Stella*)

Henderson enters from the hall

Henderson There's no need to get aggressive, my dear fellow! I'll answer your questions. (*To Stella*) I suggest you leave us, Mrs Drury. Mr Burford and I have rather a lot to talk about.

Stella hesitates, then exits

Henderson watches her, then leisurely turns towards Burford again. The two men stare at each other, Burford forcing a smile

Burford I understand you've been exchanging confidences with Mrs Drury.

Henderson Yes. I have. Amongst other things she told me about Crozier. Friend! Partner! What was your real connection with Crozier?

Burford An Italian called Victor Endrico. He worked for Crozier. We became friendly and—well, let's just say we made a successful take-over, and leave it at that.

Henderson What d'you mean, a successful take-over?

Burford I have Crozier's suitcase and Steve Kirchner is about to do business with me, not Crozier. That's what I mean, Mr Henderson.

Henderson Yes, well—I've got news for you. I don't like being conned, Mr Burford.

Burford Who does? But don't blame me. It was Crozier that invited you here. It was Crozier that lied to you about a possible film deal. However, that's all in the past. What I'm interested in is the future.

Henderson (*moving towards the bar*) I'm interested in the future too. I just want to make sure there is one so far as I'm concerned.

Burford I'm sure there is. (*Looking at him*) Well—have you reached a decision, or do you still want to sleep on it?

Henderson Yes, I've reached a decision. (*A brief pause*) It's a deal.

Burford (*pleased*) Good.

Henderson Providing we can agree on—certain things.

Burford What things?

A pause

Henderson The boy.

Burford (*surprised*) The boy?

Henderson Yes. Mrs Drury told me about her son—Mike. And what's happened to him.

Burford So?

Henderson I want you to release him.

Burford We've every intention of releasing him. Eventually.

Henderson I don't mean eventually. I mean now. Tonight.

Burford (*taken aback*) Are you serious?

Henderson Don't I sound serious?

Burford You must be out of your mind. Once we return the boy we've no hold over the Drurys. The boy will be released when you and Mrs Drury return from New York. Not until. (*Curiously*) But why are you interested in what happens to the boy?

Henderson I'm not. But I am interested in what happens to me.

Burford What's the Drury kid got to do with you?

Henderson If anything happens to Robert Drury's son there'll be a very thorough investigation. The police will discover that I stayed here and immediately jump to the conclusion that I had something to do with the kidnapping.

Burford That's nonsense! And you know it is. You must have another reason for wanting the boy set free.

Henderson What other reason could I have?

Henderson sees the dagger on the bar and, almost without thinking, picks it up

Burford (*watching him; still a shade suspicious*) All right, we'll forget the boy for the moment. What else is troubling you?

Henderson (*examining the dagger*) I don't want anyone with me. No-one. I travel alone.

Burford (*angrily*) That's out of the question! Completely out of the question!

Henderson Why?

Burford Because without Mrs Drury you could arouse suspicion. With her it'll never occur to anyone that you're not her husband.

Henderson Is that your final word—about the boy and Mrs Drury?

Burford Yes.

Henderson You're sure?

Burford I'm absolutely sure! And I'll tell you something else, my friend. If you and I don't reach an agreement—you're in trouble!

Henderson What kind of trouble?

Burford Deep trouble. You just don't understand the situation you've placed yourself in. We'd like to use you. We want to use you. But we're not, by any means, totally dependent on you.

Henderson I think you are.

Burford Then you're mistaken.

Henderson (*shaking his head*) Don't kid yourself. You can't operate without me! Who else looks like Robert Drury? Who else knows one diamond from another? I'm your lynch-pin, my friend—and you know it! (*Very sure of himself*) I want forty thousand dollars on the way to the airport and you release the boy tonight!

Burford No way! It's just not on!

Henderson (*as if to go*) Then that lets me out.

Burford I said you didn't understand the situation and you obviously don't. There's no out so far as you're concerned! You know too much. (*A brief pause*) But I'll make it thirty thousand.

Henderson And the boy?

Burford To hell with the boy! Why the boy all the time?

Henderson I've told you why. Kidnapping's not my game. Diamonds—okay. But not kids. Thirty thousand on the way to Heathrow, the boy goes free, and no Mrs Drury. I travel alone. That's it. No compromise. Take it or leave it!

Burford (*intensely angry*) No way! No bloody way at all!

Henderson Then the deal's off. We'll forget the whole thing, and I'll be on my way.

Henderson moves towards the hall. Burford's temper erupts

Burford You think it's that simple? You think I'll let you disappear—knowing what you know about the boy and the deal I've made with Steve Kirchner?

Henderson quickly turns and moves to Burford

Henderson Are you threatening me? (*Drawing nearer to him, the dagger still in his hand*) Because if you are, let me tell you something. Neither you, nor anyone else, can stop me walking out of this house and doing precisely what I want to do! And that includes shooting my mouth off, if I feel like it!

Burford backs away from the dagger

Clayton suddenly rushes in from the hall, gun in hand. He fires at Henderson, then fires again, and again

Henderson clutches his chest and staggers forward. There is blood on his hands and shirt as he falls, his body partly concealed by the sofa. Clayton dashes behind the sofa and viciously kicks Henderson's body

Clayton Bastard! Double-crossing bastard! I knew he wouldn't play! I knew damn well he'd let us down!

Burford You were right! My God, you were right! (*A brief pause*) Fetch Drury!

Clayton looks at him, hesitates, then quickly exits through the window

The telephone rings. Burford goes to the desk and lifts the receiver

Stella enters from the hall

Are you expecting a call?

Stella (*horrified, her eyes on Henderson*) What? No—no . . . (*She continues staring at Henderson*)

Burford (*on the telephone: astonished*) Victor! (*Angrily*) I told you, no out-going calls! They might trace you . . .! What's that? The boy . . .? Trouble . . .? What kind of trouble? For God's sake, he's only a kid . . .! How long has he been like this?

Stella turns, looks at Burford, then rushes towards the telephone

Stella What's happened? Is Mike ill? Let me speak to him! Please—let me speak to him!

Burford (*on the telephone, holding Stella at bay*) No, no, don't do that,
Victor . . .! How the hell should I know what to do with him? (*He looks
at Stella, still keeping her at arm's length*) Wait a minute! (*He hesitates*)
. . . I've got his mother here. Bring the boy to the phone!

Burford hands Stella the telephone

Stella (*on the telephone*) Hello . . .? (*A slight pause*) Mike . . .? Hello, my
darling! It's Mummy . . . How are you? Are you all right . . .? It's
lovely to hear your voice again . . . Are they looking after you, Mike . . .?
Yes, I know. I know, Sweetheart . . . What did Daddy say to you . . .?
We—we couldn't find Mr UFO, but don't worry, dear, we will . . .
What's that, Mike . . .? Speak up, darling, I can't hear you . . . (*Pause*)
Mike, please don't cry . . . Don't, darling! Try and be brave . . . You'll
soon be home, my darling, I promise you . . .

*Burford takes the receiver from her and slowly replaces it. Stella sinks into
the chair facing the desk, burying her face in her hands*

Stella (*distressed*) He was crying, poor darling. I—I just didn't know what
to say to him.

Burford (*quietly*) I'm sorry. I shouldn't have let you talk to him. I made a
mistake. (*Pause. He looks down at her*) Please try and control yourself.
Try and pull yourself together. You have an extremely busy day ahead
of you.

Stella looks up, staring at him in bewilderment

Within a matter of hours you'll be leaving for New York, Mrs Drury.
With your husband . . .

The Lights fade and—

the CURTAIN *falls*

SCENE 3

The same. Several hours later

*Burford is alone in the room, on the telephone to New York. He is trying to
locate Steve Kirchner and is obviously frustrated*

Burford (*on the telephone*) . . . Look, I'm sorry to trouble you but I'm
trying to get hold of a guy called Kirchner—Steve Kirchner . . .
(*Exasperated*) Yes, I know it's three o'clock in the morning in New
York everybody keeps telling me that . . . What's that . . .? He's
what . . .? Then get him *out* of bed!

Clayton rushes in from the hall

Clayton It's nearly half-past. Where are the Drurys? We should be off!
Burford They'll be down in a minute. Are the cases in the car?

Clayton nods and exits

Burford (*on the telephone*) Hello . . .? Steve . . .? Burford . . . I've had a hell of a job finding you . . .! Steve, listen—I've had to make a switch. Drury himself will contact you . . . Yes, Robert Drury . . . Yes, the *real* Robert Drury . . .! Now don't panic, everything's going to be all right . . . Drury will bring the case over, you simply go ahead as planned . . . Absolutely . . .! That's it, you've got it . . .! See you soon . . . Oh, Steve—my client from the Middle East, he knows the real thing when he sees it—so don't get any clever ideas!

Burford puts the telephone down and rises from the desk. As he does so he notices the toy—Mr UFO—and he picks it up and examines it again

Robert enters. He is carrying a document case

Is your wife ready?
Robert Not yet.
Burford Then she'd better hurry!
Robert She's in no condition to hurry. She's desperately worried about Mike.
Burford She'll be a great deal more worried about him, if you miss that plane. (*He looks at Mr UFO*) You know, something needles me about this thing. Why were you so interested in it?
Robert You said Mike had been asking for it.
Burford So?
Robert (*with a shrug*) I wondered why. It was broken. It was always going wrong.
Burford I see. (*He looks at the toy again*)

Clayton enters

Clayton Trouble!
Burford What d'you mean? What kind of trouble?
Clayton There's a woman coming up the drive—the one that showed me round the cottage.
Burford Has she seen you?
Clayton No.
Burford Don't let her see you. Keep out of her way.

Clayton nods and exits

(*To Robert, producing his gun*) Are you expecting Miss Medway?
Robert No.
Burford Then why is she coming here?
Robert I don't know. I understood she had an appointment in London this morning.
Burford We've no time to waste! Get rid of her! And get rid of her quick! *If you don't I will!*

The doorbell rings

Robert looks towards the hall, then exits. Burford goes into the office, leaving the door slightly ajar

After a little while we hear Dorothy's voice in the hall

Dorothy (*off*) I know what you're going to say, Robert! I know exactly what you're going to say! Surprise, surprise!

Dorothy enters, followed by Robert

Robert I thought you had an interview in London this morning.

Dorothy So did I. I was all ready for it. Positively quivering with anticipation. Then last night my girl friend read the letter they wrote me. You're not going to believe this, Robert! The interview's on the fourteenth of *next* month! (*Laughing*) I really think I'm going dotty! (*Moving towards the office*) Where's Stella? I haven't seen her for ages.

Robert Dorothy, I don't want to be rude, but we're both off to New York this morning, and we've got a hundred and one things to do.

Dorothy You didn't tell me you were off on another one of your trips. Is Mike going with you?

Robert No. He's staying with Mother.

Dorothy Oh, lucky Mike! I adore Italy. All those gorgeous Italians, and the food . . . (*Suddenly moving towards the office again*) Is Jane around?

Robert No, she's not! Now if you'll excuse me . . .

Dorothy Robert, I've had such an exasperating morning and no breakfast to speak of. Do you think I could pop into the kitchen and make myself a cup of black coffee?

Robert No! Dorothy you can't! I'm sorry, but you can't!

Dorothy It'll only take me five minutes and you and Stella can get on with your packing or whatever it is you've got to do.

Robert Dorothy, I'm sorry, but you've just got to go!

Dorothy Very well, Robert. (*Turning, crossing towards the hall, then hesitating*) Forgive my mentioning it again, but—have you spoken to Jane about the cheque? I had an enormous electricity bill two days ago and my bank manager . . .

Robert No, I haven't. I'll deal with it as soon as I . . . (*He has a sudden thought, looks towards the office, then turns back to Dorothy*) I'll give you the cheque now, Dorothy. Then it's done with.

Dorothy (*delighted*) Oh! Oh—thank you, my dear.

Robert goes to the desk, opens a drawer and takes out a cheque book. He picks up a pen and quickly writes a message, not just a signature, across the face of the cheque. He returns to Dorothy and hands her the cheque

Robert (*so that Burford can hear him*) Here's your cheque. You can manage on that, I hope?

Dorothy Thank you, it's very sweet of you. And I do appreciate it.

Dorothy looks at the cheque, reads what is on it, then somewhat puzzled reads it again. She stares at Robert open-mouthed, then quickly turns and gives a frightened look towards the hall and the office. Robert takes her by the arm and leads her towards the window

Dorothy exits quickly. Burford emerges from the office, gun in hand

Burford Clayton!

Clayton enters from the hall

Get outside and make sure she leaves!

Clayton nods; follows Dorothy into the garden

Burford looks at his watch

Mrs Drury should be down by now!
Robert I told you, my wife isn't at all well.
Burford If she's not down in three minutes, I'll tell Clayton to fetch her.

Stella enters. She is dressed for the flight to New York and is holding a travel bag

Stella (*quietly*) I'm ready, Robert.
Burford Good. Here's your tickets. (*He takes the tickets from his pocket and hands them to Robert*) I'll get Crozier's case.

Burford exits

A tiny pause

Robert How do you feel? Do you still feel faint?
Stella I'll be all right. Don't worry, darling. What did Dorothy want?
Robert (*softly, beckoning her to move nearer him*) I gave her a message for McKenna about New York. I said we'd stall for as long as possible.

Stella nods

We've got to play for time, Stella. We've just got to!

Burford returns. He is carrying Crozier's case

Burford The car's ready. Get your things together.
Robert (*sitting on the sofa and opening his case*) Before we leave I want to make absolutely sure that I know what it is you want us to do in New York.
Burford You know perfectly well what I want you to do. I gave you explicit instructions last night.

Robert takes a notebook out of his case and consults it

Robert We go to One-two-nine, East Forty-seventh Street?
Burford (*nodding*) My contact will be waiting for you.
Robert That's Steve Kitchener?
Burford (*impatiently*) Kirchner. He'll hand you the diamonds. (*To Stella*) You check the number, Mrs Drury. There should be twenty-four. Now remember what I told you. Take a good look at the stones. Put on a bit of an act; make the most of what you know about diamonds. (*To Robert*) You then give Kirchner the case and the following morning fly back to London. That's it! Now let's go!

Burford moves towards the hall

Robert That's not quite "it", Mr Burford. There's something you haven't told me. (*He pauses, pointing to Crozier's case*) What's in the case I'm taking to New York?

Burford If I were in your shoes, I'd rather not know. (*With a shrug*) Let's just say, it's a very special case, and leave it at that.

Robert All right. I'll put the question another way. What are the diamonds worth? Half a million? A million? Two million?

Burford You're getting warm.

Robert Then it's got to be narcotics. Heroin.

Stella (*softly; shocked*) Heroin! (*Challenging and bitter*) Do you realize what will happen if my husband's caught smuggling drugs? His career, his whole life, will be in ruins! Even if he's acquitted people will never believe he was innocent.

Burford Haven't you forgotten something? What do you think will happen to your boy if you don't take the case to New York? Do I really have to spell it out to you again? Now get moving, or you'll miss the plane!

Stella (*desperately*) No! I'm not going!

Burford stares at her for a moment

Burford (*quietly, yet with menace*) I think you are, Mrs Drury. (*He takes the gun out of his pocket*)

Stella (*approaching hysteria*) I'm not going, Robert! I'm not going to let you do this! I'm just not going to let you do it . . .

Robert moves down to Stella, takes her in his arms, holds her close to him. A long pause

Robert (*to Burford, calmly*) We'll go. We'll do what you want. But first— and I really mean this, Burford!—you've got to do something for us.

Burford (*after a moment's hesitation*) Tell me what it is—and be quick about it!

Robert My wife and I are worried, desperately worried, about the effect all this must be having on Mike.

Burford So?

Robert Let Mike come home. Let him stay here, in familiar surroundings, in his own room, until we return from the States.

There is a pause. Burford, cold, unfriendly, considers the suggestion

Stella Please, Mr Burford.

Burford No!

Robert You'll still be here, and Clayton. You'll still be holding him! For God's sake, look at the state my wife is in! What sort of a performance is she going to give on the other side of the Atlantic while she's worried to death about Mike! We'll take the case, we'll bring back the diamonds, we'll do exactly what you want—but Mike must be brought here, to the house.

A pause

Burford (*suddenly*) Okay.

Stella moves towards Burford

Stella Is that a promise?
Burford Yes. Now collect your things.
Stella How do we know you'll keep the promise?
Burford You don't. You've got to trust me. As soon as you leave I'll give instructions for the boy to be brought home.
Robert (*shaking his head*) I'm sorry, that's not good enough. You must issue the instructions now—before we leave.

Burford looks at Robert, then at Stella, hesitates—then he goes to the telephone, puts the gun down on the desk, and dials. Robert glances at his watch. There is a pause. The number is ringing out

Clayton appears

Clayton What the hell is the hold-up? We're going to miss the plane!
Burford (*puzzled*) I'm trying to get Victor! There's no reply.
Clayton Of course there's a reply! You've dialled the wrong number!

Burford replaces the receiver and, watched by Clayton, carefully dials the number again. Another pause. The number is ringing out. Stella turns to Robert; quietly takes hold of his arm. Burford stares at the telephone. The number is still ringing. Burford looks across at Robert, puzzled and worried. Robert makes no move, he stands quite still, expressionless

Burford That's bloody funny . . .

Burford continues to hold the telephone, still listening to the number ringing. Pause. In the background there is the sound of a police siren. It grows gradually louder. Robert and Stella are the first to hear the siren and turn towards the window. Clayton sees the expression on their faces, then he too hears the siren

Clayton It's the police!

Clayton exits to the hall

Burford slams down the telephone and rushes towards the window. Stella immediately realizes his mistake and dashes across to the desk and picks up the gun. Burford turns to find himself facing Stella, gun in hand. The gun is unmistakably pointing at him. Both Robert's eyes and Burford's are now on Stella

Burford Put that down! You know damn well you'll never use it!
Stella (*fiercely*) Try me, you bastard!

Burford moves a step nearer to her, then freezes. The police siren grows louder, then stops. A man's voice is heard on a loud-hailer

Man's Voice (*off*) Stay where you are, Mr Drury! We're coming in! We have your son!

Robert quickly goes to Stella and takes the gun from her

Stella rushes out into the hall crying "Mike!"

Robert stands, gun in hand. Suddenly, with his free hand, he picks up Mr UFO and throws it to Burford. Burford instinctively catches it

Robert You should have kept the pencil box, Burford. Not the toy!

CURTAIN

FURNITURE AND PROPERTY LIST

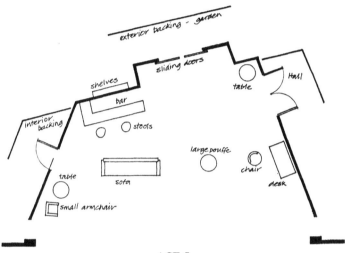

ACT I

SCENE 1

On stage: Sofa. *On it:* cushions. *On floor beside it:* small case containing portable tape-recorder and microphone, photograph

Pouffe

Desk chair

Small armchair

2 bar stools

2 occasional tables. *On them:* lamps, photographs

Desk. *On it:* telephone, desk lamp, pile of scripts, writing materials, letter opener. *In drawer:* cheque book

Bar with shelves behind. *On them:* various drinks, including Scotch, water jug, soda syphon, assorted glasses, cigarette packet containing 1 cigarette, unopened cigarette packet, lighter

Carpet

Window curtains

On walls: pictures

Off stage: Large envelope with photographs (**Jane**)

Personal: **Vivien:** wrist-watch
Robert: doorkey, wrist-watch
Stella: wrist-watch

SCENE 2

Off stage: Case. *In it:* dagger wrapped in cloth **(Burford)**
           Crozier's suitcase **(Burford)**

Personal: **Burford:** notebook, pen, wrist-watch
           Clayton: flick-knife

SCENE 3

Strike: Dirty glasses

Set: Curtains closed
           Dagger on desk
           Armchair upstage facing hall
Off stage: Long scarf **(Clayton)**

Personal: **Dorothy:** handbag
           Vivien: handbag containing gun
           Burford: car keys

ACT II

SCENE 1

Off stage: Strip of dark cloth **(Burford)**
           Pencil box, "Mr UFO space toy" **(Robert)**
           Drawing book **(Stella)**

Personal: **Robert:** small electronic device
           Clayton: length of cord

SCENE 2

Set: Armchair in original position

Check: Dagger on bar

Off stage: Loaded gun **(Clayton)**

Personal: **Clayton:** key
           Stella: handkerchief
           Henderson: blood sachet

SCENE 3

Set: Window curtains open

Check: "Mr UFO" on desk

Off stage: Document case. *In it:* notebook **(Robert)**
           Gun **(Burford)**

Personal: **Burford:** 2 air travel tickets

LIGHTING PLOT

Property fittings required: 2 table lamps, desk lamp, wall brackets
Interior. A living-room. The same scene throughout

ACT I, SCENE 1   Late afternoon

To open: General effect of fine spring day

Cue 1   **Crozier** exits   (Page 13)
             Fade to Black-out

ACT I, SCENE 2   Late afternoon

To open: As previous scene

Cue 2   **Robert:** ". . . out of the bitch!"   (Page 25)
             Fade to Black-out

ACT I, SCENE 3   Night

To open: All practicals on

Cue 3   **Robert** exits   (Page 32)
             *Fade to Black-out: return to previous lighting after short
                pause*

ACT II, SCENE 1   Night

To open: As previous scene

Cue 4   **Henderson** moves towards hall   (Page 47)
             Fade to Black-out

ACT II, SCENE 2   Night

To open: As previous scene

Cue 5   **Burford:** "With your husband. . . ."   (Page 56)
             Fade to Black-out

ACT II, SCENE 3   Early morning

To open: General effect of early spring morning light.
             All practicals off
No cues

EFFECTS PLOT

ACT I

SCENE 1

No cues

SCENE 2

Cue 1	**Stella:** "So would I." *Front doorbell rings*	(Page 16)
Cue 2	**Clayton:** "You'll what, Mr Drury?" *Pause, then telephone rings*	(Page 24)
Cue 3	**Stella** turns from **Robert** *Telephone rings*	(Page 24)

SCENE 3

Cue 4	**Robert:** "I remember wondering at the time. . . ." *Front doorbell rings*	(Page 26)
Cue 5	**Robert** moves towards bar *Telephone rings*	(Page 30)
Cue 6	**Robert:** ". . . and was surprised to find. . . ." *Telephone rings*	(Page 31)
Cue 7	**Robert:** ". . . get the operator when the phone. . . ." *Telephone rings*	(Page 31)
Cue 8	As Lights come up after Black-out *Clock chimes the hour*	(Page 32)

ACT II

SCENE 1

Cue 9	**Burford** prepares to use letter opener on toy *Front doorbell rings*	(Page 44)

SCENE 2

Cue 10	**Stella** moves away from desk *Telephone rings*	(Page 52)
Cue 11	**Clayton** exits *Telephone rings*	(Page 55)

SCENE 3

Cue 12	**Burford:** *"If you don't, I will."* *Front doorbell rings*	(Page 57)
Cue 13	**Burford:** "That's bloody funny. . . ." *Pause—then sound of police siren approaching*	(Page 61)

MADE AND PRINTED IN GREAT BRITAIN BY
LATIMER TREND & COMPANY LTD PLYMOUTH
MADE IN ENGLAND

Lightning Source UK Ltd.
Milton Keynes UK
UKOW05f0255011016

284180UK00010B/151/P